Citizen Fred:

A Nuremberg Jew's Tale

of World War II

by

Ray Scippa

with

Fred Rodell

Foreword

It was a busy day at Continental Airlines' Corporate Communications Houston offices in late January 1990. The little black carousel on the receptionist's desk was stuffed full of pink "While You Were Out" slips. When I returned from lunch at the deli, I found only one slip in my section; it had been addressed to my boss, who had crossed his name out and scribbled in mine. He knew I spoke Spanish, and the message was from the honorary consul general of Panama. Back in my office, I dialed the number on the slip. A man with a thick German accent answered. This was my first encounter with Fred Rodell.

Fred was calling to request free transportation of medical supplies to Panama in the wake of the December 1989 U.S. invasion. As honorary consul general, Fred had collected the supplies from Houston donors and was eager to deliver them in person. I could arrange that; it was one of the things I did at Continental. We agreed on a date for me to visit the consulate, meet Fred in person and see the supplies he wanted the airline to transport.

Fred greeted me at the front door to a nondescript building on Highway 6. He was a diminutive and dapper man, in a tailored dark blue suit and a tastefully colorful tie. Appearing younger than his nearly 70 years, he wore a toupee, glasses and a smile that never faded.

I arranged air transportation, and Fred delivered the supplies to Panama. When he came back he called to invite me to lunch. We went to Carmelo's Italian Restaurant on Memorial Drive, where he introduced me to the proprietor, his good friend Carmelo.

After that we spoke on the phone often. It grew into a close friendship. One day in March, I mentioned that I would be flying to Austin to attend a conference at the University of Texas. Coincidentally Fred was flying to Austin to visit his son that same day. We sat together in the first class cabin. As the flight leveled off, Fred mentioned that his next trip would be to Washington, D.C. for the 45th reunion of the Nuremberg International Military Tribunal prosecution team.

"Why are you going to that?" I asked. There was much I didn't know about my new friend, but that would soon change.

Fred explained that he had been an interrogator on the Nuremberg prosecution team. He went to all the reunions to see old friends. "You should come with me," he suggested.

I went, of course, and during the opening cocktail reception, Fred began introducing me as his biographer. This was news to me but not something I was opposed to. We discussed it on the flight home a couple of days later and settled on a plan. I would drive out to Fred's home in west Houston every Thursday evening after work. Sheryl, Fred's wife, would cook us dinner, and afterwards we would retire to his study to work on the manuscript.

I used a mini-cassette tape recorder and took copious notes on a clunky electronic word processing machine. This was a few years before my first laptop. Sometimes Fred lit up a cigarette during our sessions. That indicated an uncomfortable topic was coming, like the interludes with Colette, or the fatal encounter with two German soldiers behind enemy lines.

Our sessions went on for more than a year, and I collected all of the material that follows. Editing and rewriting ensued over the course of several more years. Fred and Sheryl moved to the Austin area to be closer to their only son, Leonard, and his family. We saw each other sporadically. On one occasion, I brought several bound copies of an early version of the manuscript to their new home in Lakeway, Texas. In October 1998, we attended an event honoring Steven Spielberg with the Lyndon Baines Johnson Moral Courage Award. Spielberg was being honored by the Holocaust Museum Houston for bringing the subject of the Holocaust to mainstream America with *Schindler's List*. On July 4, 2000, we celebrated Fred's 80th birthday with his entire family at Leonard's house. Fred and Sheryl were among the guests at my wedding on January 12, 2001.

February 20, 2005 was a typical Sunday morning. I had just sat down to read the *Houston Chronicle*. On the front page of the city section, I read about a recent murder victim from a neighborhood not far from where I lived. On a whim, I wondered if there would be an obituary for this man, whose last name began with the letter R. I turned a few pages to the death notices. That's how, completely by chance, I found Fred's obituary on the very day after he had died, the day he would be buried in the Jewish Cemetery a few miles away. I dressed quickly, got in my car and drove to Emanu El Memorial Park. As I approached the graveside, where people were already gathered beneath a white canvas tent, Leonard spotted me and rushed over to greet me. "Ray," he said, "Thank God you're here. My mother and I were trying desperately to find you."

As Leonard led me to a folding seat near the family, he said the rabbi would read from Fred's book, this book, to begin the ceremony. As I wiped away a tear for my friend, I heard the rabbi begin, "The day was July 4, 1920…"

Ray Scippa
June 2015

Timeline of Holocaust and World War II

1933 Jan. 30: President Hindenburg appoints Adolf
Hitler Chancellor of Germany
March 20: SS opens the Dachau concentration
camp outside of Munich
April 1: Boycott of Jewish-owned shops and
businesses in Germany
July 14: Law for the Prevention of Progeny with
Hereditary Diseases

1935 Sept. 15: Nuremberg Race Laws enacted
March 16: Germany introduces military
conscription

1936 March 7: German troops march unopposed into
the Rhineland
August 1: Summer Olympics begin in Berlin

1938 March 11-13: Germany incorporates Austria in
the *Anschluss* (union)
Nov. 9-10: *Kristallnacht* (nationwide pogrom in
Germany)
Sept. 29: Munich Agreement

1939 August 23: Nazi-Soviet Nonaggression Agreement
Sept. 1: Germany invades Poland, starting World
War II in Europe

Sept. 17: The Soviet Union occupies Poland from the east
Oct. 8: Germans establish a ghetto in Piotrków Trybunalski, Poland

1940   April 9: Germany invades Denmark and Norway
May 10: Germany attacks Western Europe (France and the Low Countries)
July 10: Battle of Britain begins

1941   April 6: Germany invades Yugoslavia and Greece
June 22: Germany invades the Soviet Union
July 6: *Einsatsgruppen* (mobile killing units) shoot nearly 3,000 Jews
near Kovno, Lithuania
August 3: Bishop Clemens August Graf von Galen of Münster denounces the "euthanasia" killing program in a public sermon
Sept. 28-29: *Einsatzgruppen* shoot 34,000 Jews at Babi Yar, outside Kiev, Ukraine
Nov. 7: *Einsatzgruppen* round up 13,000 Jews from the Minsk ghetto in Russia and kill them in nearby Tuchinki
Nov. 30: *Einsatzgruppen* shoot 10,000 Jews from the Riga ghetto in the Rumbula Forest
Dec. 6: Soviet winter counteroffensive
Dec. 7: Japan bombs Pearl Harbor; the U.S. declares war the next day

Dec. 8: The first killing operations begin at
Chelmno in occupied Poland
Dec. 11: Nazi Germany declares war on the
United States

1942   Jan. 16: Germans begin the mass deportation of
more than 65,000 Polish Jews from Lodz to the
Chelmno killing center
Jan. 20: Wannsee Conference held near Berlin,
Germany
March 27: Germans begin the deportation of
more than 65,000 Jews from Drancy, outside
Paris, to the east (primarily to Auschwitz)
June 28: Germany launches a new offensive
towards the city of Stalingrad
July 15: Germans begin mass deportations of
nearly 100,000 Jews from the Occupied
Netherlands to the east (primarily to Auschwitz)
July 22: Germans begin the mass deportation of
over 300,000 Jews from the Warsaw ghetto to the
Treblinka killing center
Sept. 12: Germans complete the mass deportation
of about 265,000 Jews from Warsaw to Treblinka
Nov. 23: Soviet troops counterattack at
Stalingrad, trapping the German Sixth Army in
the city

1943   April 19: Warsaw ghetto uprising begins
July 5: Battle of Kursk

Oct. 1: Rescue of Jews in Denmark
Nov. 6: Soviet troops liberate Kiev
March 19: German forces occupy Hungary

1944   May 15: Germans begin the mass deportation of 440,000 Jews from Hungary
June 6: D-Day: Allied forces invade Normandy, France
June 22: Soviets launch an offensive in eastern Belorussia (Belarus)
July 25: Anglo-American forces break out of Normandy
Aug. 1: Warsaw Polish uprising begins
Aug. 15: Allied forces land in southern France
Aug. 25: Liberation of Paris
Dec. 16: Battle of the Bulge

1945   Jan. 12: Soviet winter offensive
Jan. 18: Death march of nearly 60,000 prisoners from Auschwitz camp
Jan. 25: Death march of nearly 50,000 prisoners from the Stutthof camp in Poland
Jan. 27: Soviet troops liberate the Auschwitz camp complex
March 7: U.S. troops cross the Rhine River at Remagen
April 16: Soviets launch their final offensive, encircling Berlin

April 29: American forces liberate the Dachau concentration camp

April 30: Adolf Hitler commits suicide in his bunker in Berlin

May 7: Germany surrenders to the Western Allies

May 9: Germany surrenders to the Soviets

Sept. 2: Japan surrenders. World War II officially ends

Nov. 20: The International Military Tribunal, made up of U.S., British, French and Soviet judges, begins a trial of 22 major Nazi leaders at Nuremberg, Germany

1946   Oct. 1: The International Military Tribunal passes judgment on major Nazi war criminals. Eighteen are convicted and three acquitted. Eleven are sentenced to death

Oct. 16: Ten of the Nuremberg defendants are executed by hanging. One defendant, Hermann Göring, commits suicide in his cell

Fred's Prologue
Euthanasia in Nazi Germany

It was the spring of 1987. I was driving from Munich to Stuttgart on the autobahn to visit my cousin Julius. I had a little rented Opel. After I left Munich, in the late afternoon, it started to rain in torrential sheets. It was dark, and people kept passing me at high speed. Even with my windshield wipers going full blast, the backsplash from cars passing me made it impossible to see. Anyhow, I don't see very well anymore at night.

Better than halfway to Stuttgart, I decided to get off the autobahn and find a place to stay for the night. In the little resort town of Bad Überkingen, I saw a sign for a restaurant and rooms. By then it was nearly 10 p.m. The proprietor showed me to a spotlessly clean, newly furnished room with all the amenities. I told him I'd take it and asked if the restaurant was still open. It was, so I cleaned up and went to the restaurant, which was empty except for one elderly gentleman sitting at a table.

I ordered wienerschnitzel. While waiting for my food, I started to read a local newspaper. The man sitting nearby, drinking his beer, obviously wanted to make conversation. He spoke to me in English, "Have you come to this town for the mineral baths?"

Looking over my paper, I replied in German, my native language, "No. I'm just driving through on my way to Stuttgart from Munich."

The man smiled, realizing I was not a typical tourist. He introduced himself and I told him I was Fred Rodell from Houston, Texas, formerly Fred Rosenfeld of Nuremberg.

"I come here every year since the end of the war for the baths," he said. "They're invigorating. It's a great spa."

We made small talk for some time. At one point, he said, "This is really a sad day for me."

"Why is that?"

"It is the anniversary of my only brother's death."

"I'm very sorry to hear that," I said. "Was he involved in an accident?"

"Oh, no, nothing like that. It's a very old, very sad story. You see, he had a mental disorder and was institutionalized because he was schizophrenic. But that's not the whole story."

I could see that, as painful as the story was for him, the man wanted to tell me everything, so I nodded for him to go on.

"One evening, before the end of the war, a Nazi storm trooper knocked on our front door. When I opened the door, he presented me with an urn that he told me contained my brother's ashes. He also handed me an envelope, saying, quite curtly, that my brother had died in the institution. As if that was all the *explanation I deserved, he clicked his heels together, gave the Nazi salute and left.*

"I was completely dumbfounded, because we hadn't heard from my brother in weeks and had no idea that he might have been ill. I took the urn, put it on a small table in the hallway and then opened the envelope. Inside I found a death certificate; it listed the cause of death as peritonitis due to the bursting of his appendix. I knew this could not be true since I remembered very well that many years before my brother was institutionalized, he had trouble with his appendix and it was removed."

The man stopped to finish off his stein of beer and motion to the waiter for another. I asked him, "Where was the institution where your brother was staying?"

"It was a small institution not far outside Munich."

"Egelfing-Haar?" I asked, knowing he would say yes.

"How did you know?"

"And the certificate was signed by a Doctor Hermann Pfannmüller."

The man was intrigued. "How could you know this? Who are you? Were you hospitalized there too?"

"No, I just know a lot about this particular institution and Doctor Pfannmüller."

The man leaned forward and caught my eyes in his own. "Why?"

I took a deep breath. It had been many years since I had spoken of my experiences, but the memories were as fresh as if only days had passed. I responded, "You see, I'm an American. After my military service with the U.S. Army, I became a member of the prosecution staff of the International Military Tribunal at

14

Nuremberg. I worked as well on what were called the Subsequent Proceedings. One of those cases I worked on was the case against the medical establishment in Nazi Germany. My particular role in that case was to interrogate doctors who were involved in the so-called euthanasia program carried out during the Third Reich."

I could see that my new acquaintance was both horrified and attracted by this unexpected opportunity to hear more about his brother's murder. For that was indeed what it was and what he had suspected for so many years. I spoke with him long into the night; he wouldn't let me go to bed until I had told him all about Pfannmüller, whom I had interrogated many times. His brother had been but one of the millions of victims of the Nazi euthanasia program, and his anguished questions brought back to my memory in startling detail, the whole terrible story.

The man in Bad Überkingen didn't even know what euthanasia meant. I explained that it was a Greek word that means "good death." He scoffed at the very idea. The practice began in Nazi Germany in 1940 with the elimination of what the Nazis called "useless eaters," to free up hospital beds for the war effort. The first to go were, ironically, German World War I veterans who were basket cases, without limbs. They could produce nothing for the Third Reich. Since they occupied beds that would be needed for soldiers of the present war, they were quickly branded as useless eaters.

The next phase was people considered incurably ill. Again they occupied beds, produced nothing and hence were useless eaters. As time went along it became easier and easier for the Third Reich to justify adding more groups into the euthanasia program. Before long, children with only slight deformities were being systematically liquidated.

In the end, it was no longer called euthanasia, as it spread to the mass killing of Gypsies and Jews, Poles, Czechs and Russians, anyone who resisted the Nazi war machine. Instead we know it now as the Holocaust.

"Pfannmüller was nothing more than a murderer," the man murmured.

"That's true," I agreed. "But he never stopped denying it."

During my interrogation of Doctor Pfannmüller, I vividly recall asking him whether he killed children. He said, "No, I did not kill them."

I told him that we had it on good authority that he gave them injections.

"That's right," he answered.

"Was the purpose of those injections to kill them?"

"No, I didn't kill them."

"What kind of injections were these?"

"Morphine and scopolamine."

"What effect did they have on the children?"

His answer was, "They went to sleep."

"Well," I pressed him, "Did they ever wake up?"

After a long pause, he answered, "No."

"In other words, you gave them an overdose of morphine and scopolamine that killed them."

He paused again before answering. "We gave it to them to quiet them down, to make them rest."

When I finished my story in Bad Überkingen, it was obvious that the man was shaken. He said to me, "For years since the end of the war we've heard stories like this and I would never believe them. I was a loyal party member. I knew there was something suspicious about my brother's death, but I assumed someone had made an honest mistake on the death certificate. Even though it bothered me, there was no way for me to verify it. Now, I know better. You made me realize what really happened to my brother and millions more like him."

"That's all so far behind us now," I said, suddenly feeling that I had caused this man some terrible anguish.

"Just to think that I supported the terrible regime that murdered my brother."

It was already 2 a.m. when I walked the man to the door. As we started to say goodbye, he suddenly grabbed my arm and asked, "Whatever happened to Pfannmüller?"

"He was too small a fry to be tried at Nuremberg. He was a witness for the prosecution, nothing more, just a cog in the wheel. He was probably tried by a smaller military court."[1]

Before we parted, the man took my hand in both of his and thanked me for clearing up a mystery that had plagued him since the day he received his brother's ashes.

"Thank God that period in our history is over," he said.

"Yes," I agreed, "Thank God."

---

[1] Pfannmuller testified at the Nuremberg trials that "...euthanasia and the work of the National Board had, in my view, nothing to do with National Socialism. They were just as legal as the regulations for prevention of transmission of hereditary diseases and infection in marriage. These laws were passed during the National Socialist Regime. But the ideas from which they arose are centuries old." In 1948, he was declared unfit to stand trial. The next year he was sentenced to six years in jail. Pfannmüller died in 1961 in Munich at the age of 75.

PART ONE

Growing up in Nuremberg and New York

Chapter One

The day was July 4, 1920. It was early afternoon on the East Coast of the United States, where people were enjoying their Independence Day holiday. But at Heideloffplatz 15 in Nuremberg, Germany, utter confusion reigned. Frieda Rosenfeld was about to deliver her first child after 14 years of marriage. Her doctor, Herr Wasserman, wanted her to check into the hospital to deliver, but her husband Leopold violently objected.

"No, no, no!" he said, shaking a fist in the air. "No hospital. What if they exchange the baby by mistake, what then, huh? My son will be born right here under my own roof!"

Leopold won the argument and, amidst much excitement, Fred Rosenfeld was born in his family's luxury apartment surrounded by relatives and friends.

His early years were filled with family. Uncle Max and Uncle Siegfried were constantly at their home. So was Aunt Rosa Mannheimer, her husband Henry and their son Rudy, who was six months older than Fred. The Heideloffplatz apartment was a meeting place for them all, a place to eat and laugh together in those last years before the world turned very dark.

Fred was particularly fond of his older cousin Irma and her husband Dolf. When they came with their daughter Margot, there was music in the air. Cousin Irma was very beautiful, and Fred watched her float from room to room with the kind of adoration young boys secretly reserve for older female relatives.

Everyone visited each other often. They traveled as far as Munich to see Leopold's side of the family, cousin Louie Holtzer, his wife and their first born daughter, just a few months younger than Fred. It was a very close family that did everything together.

Leopold Rosenfeld was a very religious man. Every Friday afternoon, he would close his business early, hurry home to change his clothes, and take his wife and son to Friday night services in the synagogue. He had a regular seat there, and Fred sat right next to him, trying to follow the service so his father would be proud of him.

The first office I remember my father having was on the ground floor of an apartment building that he owned at Glockenhofstrasse 39. I remember being very impressed — at the age of four or five — that he had a motorcycle right smack in the middle of his office. And around it was a bunch of medals and awards. It seemed that, prior to my birth, my father was an ardent motorcycle racer and won

20

many contests. After I was born, my mother objected to his sport, and he stopped for her and me.

Leopold Rosenfeld owned and operated a clothing factory in Nuremberg. He manufactured suits, coats and overcoats sold by fashionable retail stores throughout Germany. During the early twenties, Leopold's business did well and was recognized around the country. His family remained prosperous through the lingering German depression.

Then, in 1928, Leopold fell ill with chronic heart trouble. At first, he went to a sanatorium in Ebenhausen, near Munich. He went from one doctor to another. His blood pressure was quite high; as treatments, they put leeches on him and made controlled cuts in his veins to relieve the pressure.

By 1929, Leopold was completely bedridden, and his wife had to step in and run the business. It was difficult for her to do that and at the same time care for an ailing husband. So, in 1930, they turned the business over to Leopold's brother David, who was living in Frankfurt. He came to Nuremberg with his wife Ella and a son, Lothar, several years younger than Fred.

In October 1931, Leopold Rosenfeld finally passed on. Fred, who had been so close to his father, was devastated. On the day, his mother awakened Fred early, knowing the time was near and wanting the boy to be out of the house when it came. She gave him money to go to the local fair, and he went, unaware of what was happening. It was a typical harvest fair, no better or worse than any other he had ever attended, but it kept him entertained until early evening.

When I came home, the first room I went to was my father's bedroom. Not realizing that he had already passed away, I climbed into bed with him, because he always told me that he could sleep better if my chin was next to his chin. About twenty minutes passed like that before Aunt Rosa came in and dragged me out of there. She told me that my father would never wake up again. With my head in her apron, I sobbed for hours.

But life went on, on into a different time. Frieda Rosenfeld continued, buoyed by the love and affection of her two bachelor brothers Max and Siegfried, who were constantly by her side. Fred grew up, attending the public middle school.

Nuremberg had become a dangerous place for Jews long before Hitler came into power in 1933. Beginning in the early 1930s the Nazi party leader for Nuremberg, Julius Streicher, held sway. Among his activities was the publication of the highly anti-Semitic newspaper *Der Stürmer*.[2] A division

---

[2] In 1923, Streicher established his anti-Semitic newspaper, Der Stürmer (The Stormtrooper). In the same year, Streicher took part in Adolf Hitler's abortive Beer Hall Putsch. Following Hitler's release from prison, he named Streicher his Gauleiter (district leader) of Middle Franconia. In his capacity as chair of the Central Committee to Repulse Jewish Atrocity and Boycott Agitation (*Zentralkomitee zur Abwehr der jüdischen Greuel- und Boykotthetze*), he helped to organize the famous one-day boycott of Jewish businesses on April 1, 1933. In May 1945, Streicher was captured by US forces, and convicted on the charge of crimes against humanity in a trial of major war criminals before the International Military Tribunal at Nuremberg. He was hanged in Nuremberg, his former stronghold, on October 16, 1946.

between Jew and German had been drawn; hostility was brewing on the streets of the city.

Fred had many friends in his classes at the normal school. Before 1933, he never experienced anti-Semitism, and neither did his family. One of his father's friends at the Ebenhausen Sanatorium was the famous steel magnate Thyssen. He had warned Leopold to get out of Germany, saying it would be very bad for Jews because the Nazis would eventually come to power. Later, Fred would find out that Thyssen had helped to finance the Nazi party.

While he was growing up, the boy experienced Germany slowing emerging from its terrible post-World War I depression. He remembered times when the elder Rosenfeld would have to go to the country to trade clothing for food, so that his family could get the things they needed to eat. Beggars would often come to the door. Frieda fed them soup or meat, whatever she had. People were hungry. Fred looked out the window and saw people singing in the street. His mother opened the window and threw coins down to them. Unemployment was very high, an enormous difficulty for people in Germany at that time that perhaps helped the Nazi party rise more than anything.

Before they came into power, the Nazis promised work for all. Everyone would earn money and could buy whatever they needed. No one realized the work they were talking about would be in the military or labor camps.

On July 15, 1933, the family celebrated Fred's bar

mitzvah. [3] Two days later, on Monday, July 17, the doorbell rang early in the morning. Fred, still in his pajamas, watched the maid open the door. Some Nazi party members came in asking: "Where's the man of the house?"

"I am the man of the house," Fred answered. After all, his rabbi told him only two days earlier that he was bar mitzvah, and therefore, he was a man – the only man in this household.

The men shoved the maid aside, ignoring Fred, and started searching from room to room. First they came to a guest bedroom, where Aunt Lena was sleeping. They woke her up and asked her where her man was. She said there was no man. Then they went to Aunt Rosa's room, another guest room. And finally, they entered Frieda's room. She explained to them that she was a widow, her husband had died in October 1931.

They were convinced enough to leave. After they were gone, the women and Fred looked out through the curtains and saw how Jewish men were being dragged out of their houses into the street in their underclothes or nightclothes, or whatever they had on. They were being marched off. No one knew where they were going.

Fred dressed quickly and took his most prized bar mitzvah gift, a new bicycle, out into the courtyard, which was enclosed by a seven-foot wall. He managed to hoist the bike up

[3] On Jan. 30, 1933, President Hindenburg appointed Adolf Hitler Chancellor of Germany. On March 20, the SS opened the Dachau concentration camp outside of Munich. On April 1, the boycott of Jewish-owned shops and businesses was launched in Germany.

and over the wall and scrambled after it. On the back street there were no Storm Troopers. Fred rode quickly to Uncle David's house and warned him to go and hide somewhere.

On his way back home, Fred encountered a friend, Fritz Gutman, who lived next door. "The brown shirts have taken all the Jewish men they could find to the stadium," he said. "Let's take our bikes and go there!"

"Wait," Fred said, "First let's go home and get some food for them."

So the two boys went to the Rosenfeld kitchen and made sandwiches of white cheese on thick slices of bread. They wanted to feed as many of the men as they could. At the stadium, they couldn't believe what they saw. All the men were down on their knees, their arms behind their backs, cutting the grass with their teeth and spitting it out. A guard stopped the boys and asked them what they wanted.

"We've brought lunch," they said. "It's noon."

The guard put his hand on Fred's head and said quietly, "Don't worry son, they'll be home soon. You can tell your mothers not to worry. Just go right home, don't watch this."

I was worried about Uncle Max until I learned that one of his friends, a postal worker with whom he served in World War I, had gotten advance notice of the Nazi action. He took a postal van to my uncle's home at 3:30 in the morning, woke him up and told him what was going to take place. He ordered Uncle Max to get in the back of the van, and then he piled boxes over him and drove him out of town.

It was 1934, on the day of the normal school's annual sports festival — a full-day event with track and field, handball and soccer. The highlight of the day was the soccer game between the two leading school teams. Fred was on one of the teams.

Before his big game, he sat in the stands watching a handball game. A classmate came to him and said, "Rosenfeld, you better get out of here fast."

Fred thought he had taken someone's seat, so he got up and went to the back seats to watch the game from the last row, standing. Suddenly, someone pulled his arms up from behind, making him bend forward. He turned his head to see who it was and saw the uniform of an SA man (*Sturmabteilung*, or Storm Trooper) for only a split second before he got a fist to the left side of his face. His head swung around and was met by another fist to the right side of his face.

The SA men escorted Fred to the stadium steps, fifteen stone steps leading to the field level where Fred had been sitting only moments before. They stopped at the top, long enough for Fred to see the faces of the crowd watching, some frozen in terror, others hiding their reactions. Suddenly, Fred felt a boot in the middle of his back, sending him tumbling down the length of the steps. At the bottom, he lay unconscious.

Other Jewish boys picked him up and carried him home. His mother was not at home, so a neighbor took him to the hospital. He remembered nothing of any this when he woke up. For the next three weeks, he lay in traction in the hospital. Initially, the doctors believed he would never walk again. His hip was badly injured. They were wrong.

He did walk again, with a slight limp at first, and later as if nothing had ever happened. He would feel pain in the hip from time to time even years later as an old man, but the most significant scar from this episode was in Fred's mind. He learned that the reason for the assault was the fact that for the final soccer game that day, Julius Streicher was to be in attendance. The party leader had sent his men ahead to clear the stadium of all Jews before he entered. His orders were followed to a tee.

Fred's total recuperation in the hospital and at home lasted more than three months. Frieda went to the school to complain to the principal.

"What do you expect?" he told her, shrugging. "After all, your son is a Jew."

Frieda withdrew Fred from the normal school and enrolled him in the Jewish Middle School in Furth. (The school's most famous alumnus was Henry Kissinger.) In 1936, Frieda decided to send Fred away to a school in Milan, Italy. By that time, the boy had decided to study radio and electrical engineering. She picked Italy because, thanks to Hitler's pact with Mussolini, it was the only country to which she could legally send money. Under Hitler's rule, Germany had all sorts of money restrictions.

Another reason to send Fred to Milan was because Cousin Irma and her husband Dolf were living there. They would be able to keep an eye on him. In order for him to learn Italian as quickly as possible, however, it was decided that Fred should not stay with his relatives but with a local family that spoke only Italian. So it was that Fred Rosenfeld, a Jewish boy from Nuremberg, came to live with the family of a Milanese certified public accountant by the name of Renato Raddi.

Chapter Two

Signore Raddi lived with his wife, two children and mother-in-law in a small but comfortable apartment near downtown Milan. As an honored and paying guest, Fred was given an entire room and treated like a long lost relative come home at last.

They were delightful people, but I had a terrible time in the beginning. I couldn't communicate with anyone. I remember going to the dinner table night after night, eating as fast as I could, and then going back to my room. Many, many times I cried myself to sleep like a baby.

In school, the other students made fun of his accent. They told him to say certain words to the professor, which he would repeat only to find out later that they were mostly vulgar or insults. The experience had one redeeming quality: Fred applied himself to learning Italian in record time.

Then a new world opened up to him. The formerly obedient and decorous lad turned wild. Having learned the language and being completely on his own for the first time with a substantial sum of money always at his disposal, Fred discovered the finer things of life. His mother sent him a total of 1,500 lire every month. With it he paid his room and board of less than 500 lire to Raddi, whose monthly salary was only 1,000 lire. Raddi supported a wife, two children and a mother-in-law on that amount. Back in Nuremberg, Frieda was certain that there was no way her son could possibly spend all the money she sent. She expected him to put much of it in a savings account. How wrong Frieda was.

I rented motorcycles at first and learned to race through the streets of Milan, imagining how my father had felt racing around a track. Suddenly girls took on a more important position in my life. I found myself surrounded by dark-eyed and shy Italian beauties. For them, I quickly graduated to renting cars and cutting classes to take them on trips into the magnificent Italian countryside. When the weather was warm, I took them to the beach near Genoa. In the winter, I took them skiing at Alpine resorts.

One day in early spring, Fred received a call from his mother, telling her that she'd be arriving the next morning in Milan. He went to meet her at the train station. After hugging and kissing him, she said, "I'm not going to stay in Milan long,

Fred. You have your school to attend, and I don't want to interfere with your studies. I'll be going to spend two weeks on the Riviera, and you can come to visit on the weekends."

"That sounds wonderful, Mother," Fred said, smiling.

"The only problem is that they wouldn't permit me to take any foreign currency when I left Germany. So, we'll have to go to your bank and withdraw some of the money I've been sending you."

Fred's smile faded quickly. "But mother, I haven't got a bank account."

Frieda looked surprised, then perplexed. "Where have you put the money?"

Fred began to squirm. A terrible sense of guilt swept over him, and he confessed with tears in his eyes to having blown nearly every penny of the money his mother had sent. He reached into his pocket and pulled out a wad of bills, less than 200 lire.

Frieda was mortified, but she didn't shout or strike him. She just stood there surrounded by the hubbub of the Milan train station. Her shoulders slumped as she gradually accepted the only choice left to her.

"I cannot stay here now," she said, looking at Fred sadly. "There is a train back to Germany in twenty minutes. I'll have to go."

Half an hour later his mother was gone. Fred walked through the streets back to the apartment, his head hanging. By the time he reached home, he made up his mind. He gathered up his school books and marched off to school, determined to turn over a new leaf of responsibility.

Fred grew to truly love Italy and the Italians. The most blessed memories he gathered in his youth date to the time he spent in Milan. He became very active in sports, even joining the Italian ski team. One of his closest friends was Edoardo Mangiarotti, the world champion fencer who, in 1936, won the gold medal for fencing at the Berlin Olympics. In fact, Edoardo took the gold from his brother, who had it turn taken it from their father. Since 1904 in St. Louis, Missouri, through eight Olympic Games, the gold medal for fencing had resided with the Mangiarotti family.

Life among his friends in Italy was good, perhaps too good to go on in the world as it was in those years before the war. In 1938, at the height of Fred's time in Milan, when he was happier than ever before, Mussolini passed a law whereby all Jews who came to Italy after 1918 were compelled to leave within six months. Although the thought of leaving Italy saddened him, fortunately, for Fred, Frieda had had the foresight to apply much earlier for an entry visa to the United States. She had long planned for the entire family to immigrate as soon as Fred's studies were completed. Now the boy would have to go alone.

But first he had to go to Germany. In August, Fred received a telegram from his mother telling him that the U.S. Consulate in Stuttgart wanted him to present himself for an interview regarding his visa request. The news made him very happy until the next day. A German friend, whose name coincidentally happened to be Alfred Rosenfeld, a fellow student who lived with an Italian family in the apartment just above Fred's, had also been called to Stuttgart for an interview.

He told Fred that when his train stopped at the German border, the Nazi officials asked him how long he had been out of Germany.

"When I told them two years, they offered me a choice," he said. "To return to Italy, or to go to what they called a reorientation center in Germany."

Wisely, the boy had opted to return to Milan.

Now Fred had to decide. That evening, sitting in his room and listening to the talk and laughter of the Raddi family in the next room, Fred pondered his dilemma. He had to get to Stuttgart by the 29th, but the moment he entered Germany, they would put him in a camp and he would certainly miss his appointment if not worse. In the dim light, his restless eyes suddenly focused on the uniform hanging behind his door. Along with his school tuition, he was required to join the Student Fascist Organization, a requirement he despised. They had even given him this uniform.

Fred packed the uniform at the top of his valise, thinking that when the German border guards searched his belongings, they would see it and leave him alone. It was the only thing he could think of to do.

Early the next morning as he set off on foot for the station, Fred fell in beside a fellow from the Academy, an ambitious young man from a local working-class family, who called himself Captain Basevi and was proud to be one of the Student Fascist officers. The affable, round-faced youth had not fully grasped the true meaning of the organization. He was a studious engineering student, and had no idea that Fred was Jewish, nor did he care.

"Going to the station too?" he asked cheerfully.

"Yes, I'm on my way to Germany," Fred replied.

"Oh, you must also be a delegate to the Nazi Party Congress in Nuremberg. That's where I'm off to. Is that it?"

Fred shook his head no. They had arrived at the wrought iron gateway in front the Milano train station. Basevi held the gate open for Fred, smiling a wide, happy smile.

As it turned out, they were traveling on the same train. Fred would go straight through to Stuttgart; Basevi had to change trains once they crossed the German border. They sat together, the sole occupants of a small compartment. There was a slight delay before the train lurched forward. Through the window, Fred could soon see the northern Italian countryside he loved so much. The thought of leaving it, even to go to America, saddened him. Basevi kept up a good-natured banter about everything and anything. The closer they came to the German border, the less Fred listened. He began to sweat, and he had to hold his hands together in his lap to keep from shaking.

Finally, Basevi touched his arm and said, "Fred, what's with you? You look terrible."

Fred needed to talk. He told Basevi he was a Jew and explained what had happened to his friend, the other Fred Rosenfeld.

Basevi frowned. "It's too bad I don't have an extra uniform that would fit you. You could put it on and say that you were with me."

Fred remembered the uniform in his own valise. Of course, he must put it on. There was no other way.

"Let's see it," Basevi said. And when Fred held up an identical student fascist uniform to the one he was wearing, the Captain threw up his hands. "Put it on, immediately!" he said.

Basevi stood watch outside the door to the compartment as Fred changed into the uniform. About 30 minutes later, the train stopped at the border. Two Nazi officials entered the boys' compartment and gave them the Nazi salute. The boys returned the gesture, Basevi with unbridled enthusiasm, Fred feeling a mixture of self-consciousness and horror. One of the officials seemed to notice and stared at Fred for a moment. Then they walked out.

The boys sat in silence for several minutes. Fred felt his heart still pounding in his chest; he was waiting for the suspicious guard to appear again looking for him. Suddenly the shrill train whistle sounded and the train lurched forward again. Basevi laughed and pounded Fred on the back. But that was not quite all there was to it.

At the next station, Basevi had to change trains. He bid Fred goodbye, still chuckling over their success. Many people were getting on the train, and Fred watched several squeeze into the compartment. Having crossed into Germany without trouble, he now faced a big problem. How would he get out of the fascist uniform that, although it had saved him, he still despised? There were now five Germans sitting around him in the compartment.

I sat and kept silent, pretending I did not speak German. They smiled, I smiled, but no conversation. The train pulled into Stuttgart station, and feeling like a traitor to my people, I stepped out, onto the platform. Standing not fifteen feet away, my mother and Uncle Max saw me at the same moment. Uncle Max had to grip my mother's arm to keep her from falling backward at the sight of me.

They were to spend the night at Aunt Rosa's house in Cannstadt. Frieda, Uncle Max and Fred took the streetcar. When Uncle Max attempted to pay the conductor, he refused to accept any money for their tickets, shaking his head and saying, "Italian storm troopers ride for free in Germany."

By the time they reached Aunt Rosa's house it was dark. They stood on her porch and Fred stepped forward to ring the bell. Inside Aunt Rosa peeked through a side window and felt a wave of panic. All she could see was the silhouette of a man in uniform.

The next day, dressed in a nice business suit, Fred went with Frieda to the U.S. Consulate. After the usual questioning, he was granted permission to immigrate to the United States.

Chapter Three

From Stuttgart, they returned to Nuremberg. Fred was to spend several weeks at home, then go back to Milan, get his things together, and take a ship to the United States. Frieda would follow in about 30 days, when she had secured her own visa. Plans, however, don't always work out as intended.

"You need a haircut, Fred," Frieda said, two days after their arrival in Nuremberg.

Fred and his Uncle Max were sitting at the kitchen table, having just finished a lunch of Frieda's delicious beef stew. Uncle Max looked at the boy's curly brown hair and nodded his agreement. "Yes," he said, "You should go to see Feivel."

Frieda pulled some money from her pocketbook and stuffed it into his hand. "Go this afternoon, while I have some errands to run."

Feivel, the barber, whose little shop was just two blocks away on Heideloffplatz, had cut Fred's hair since his first haircut. He was very busy that day. As Fred waited, a young man entered and asked if he could have his hair cut immediately. "I've been called to active duty," he explained to Feivel. "I must leave at once."

As Fred continued to wait, several more men came in, all with the same urgency to get a haircut, all saying they too had been called to active duty. Fred gave up waiting, slipped out of the crowded shop and went home.

When Uncle Max heard what had happened, he rose from his chair in the living room with a look of alarm. "Dear God," he said, "Germany is starting a war."

He walked quickly to the front window and looked out as if he might see something right there on the sleepy middle class street. "We've got to get you out of the country immediately. If the war starts, they'll never let you leave! Go pack your things." He turned to look at Fred. The alarm had been replaced with a deep sadness in his eyes. "It's very urgent, Fred. I'll take you to the train station. We can't even wait for your mother to get home."

Fred could not believe what was happening. He packed slowly, hoping his mother would come home before they left. But Uncle Max came into his room and made him hurry. In less than half an hour, they were at the train station. Uncle Max purchased a ticket to Milan via Switzerland. "Listen, Fred," he said, gravely grasping the boys' hands in his own. "I'm going to give you some instructions that you must carry out. At every station, I want you to buy a newspaper. If war should break out, and Italy is involved, you must stay in Switzerland." He took a pen and hurriedly wrote the name of his friend in

Zurich on the jacket of Fred's train ticket. "Call him and he will help you," Uncle Max said.

Fred did as he was instructed, buying newspapers in each station along the route to Italy. While the news was not good, the war did not break out, so he continued on to his room in Milan.

My mother was very upset that she couldn't even say goodbye to me, but it was for the best. Since my mother could pay the ocean fare with German marks, she got me a first class reservation on the S.S. Washington, which would leave on October 6 from Le Havre, France. Meanwhile, I packed all my belongings and had a good time with my friends.

Back in Nuremberg, Frieda cried when she came home to find her son gone. She knew Max had done the right thing, but she cried in front of him anyway, wrenching his heart. The truth was that war was imminent. Everyone in Germany knew it by now.

In Italy, however, Fred was not so aware. Toward the end of September, his German-Jewish friends began to slip away, one by one. One evening, he called his cousin Irma, only to find out that she, Dolf, the children and even the maid had already left for Switzerland.

When I heard this news, I decided not to go to Switzerland, but to go directly to France. After all, my ship left from there, and I had never been to gay Paris. I figured it would be fun to spend the week there. I bought a ticket, sent a telegram to a cousin of mine in Paris, telling him to meet me in the train station, and off I went.

The world news grew increasingly worse as Fred traveled to France. World War II was indeed imminent. Sitting on the train, passing some of the world's greatest scenery, a jumble of thoughts swept through his mind.

I knew I was sailing in uncharted waters — all alone, not knowing what was ahead. When would I see my mother again? What would become of me? I was leaving old friends behind. Now I missed even the Raddi family in their apartment. Again, I was going to a country whose language I didn't speak.

The train stopped at the Italian-French border. Two Italian customs officials examined Fred's passport, then one of them politely requested that he leave the train and follow them into the nearby customs building. Once inside a small bare room, they asked him to remove all of his clothing. As he was pulling off his shirt, another man entered with his luggage. The two officials thoroughly examined the contents of Fred's suitcase while he stood to one side completely naked. Finding nothing in the luggage, they turned their attention to Fred again.

I was asked to bend over and cough and my rectum was checked for hidden diamonds, gold or other items of value. Oh, they were perfectly polite about it, and probed quite delicately, but my ears and necked burned with the humiliation of it.

Fred dressed alone in the little room, then returned to his train compartment as he had been told. The train moved slowly across the border. On the other side, as a French official checked the papers of each passenger, men with buckets of paint began to paint all the train's windows black. Once they were finished, the train continued and arrived in Paris several hours later. The City of Lights was experiencing its first complete blackout.

When Fred saw his cousin Harold waiting at the station, he started right in saying how sorry he was that he would be imposing on them for a week while he waited in Paris for his ship, the S.S. Washington, to sail.

Harold looked puzzled. "Didn't you get the telegrams we sent?"

"What telegrams?"

"From your mother in Germany and me. Even the ship sent you notification. You've got to be on board today. The sailing has been moved up a week because of the war situation."

Fred had received no cables. He had been lucky to leave Milan when he did. If he had waited even a day, he would have missed the boat. The two young men went directly from the Paris train station to Le Havre, where Fred boarded the S.S. Washington that night. Everyone on board was talking about the Munich Conference. Even though his mother had purchased him a first class ticket, he had to share his cabin with three other people. The ship was overcrowded because the U.S.

Government had recalled the families of American diplomats.

The ship set sail from Le Havre on September 30. Its first port of call was Southampton, England. As it docked there, word spread quickly throughout the ship that British Prime Minister Neville Chamberlain had returned to London from Munich with the famous announcement: "We have achieved peace for our time."

All the Americans who had been recalled were taken off the ship and returned to their posts on the continent. I had my cabin to myself again. As the ship left Southampton, the purser's office opened, which meant I could withdraw the $50 the German government had permitted me to take out of Germany. In my mind everything seemed to be going right again. There would be no war, so my family would be safe left behind in Germany, and I was embarking on a great adventure.

Since there were many refugees on board the Washington, the line in front of the purser's office was very long. Everybody wanted their money. Fred decided to wait until the line subsided and take a walk around deck to familiarize himself with the ship. Before he had gone far, he came face to face with his cousin, Leo Strass. It was a great reunion. They had no idea they were on the same ship until the moment they saw each other on deck. Leo had been hurrying to get in line for his $50, but after embracing Fred several times, he led him back to his cabin to see his wife, Bertha, and their infant daughter, Leni.

At last I didn't feel so all alone. During the week-long transatlantic crossing, I spent a lot of time with my cousins, and I was fascinated by their little baby Leni.

That first afternoon, Fred was thoroughly amused when his cousin Leo went to get his $50. He waited in line, but by the time he got to the window, he became seasick and had to rush to the rail without getting his money. He had to start all over from the rear of the line. That happened to poor Leo several times.

After Fred received his money, he discovered that the ship was equipped with slot machines, a toy he had never experienced before.

By the time I reached New York, I had invested a total of $49.75. Upon my arrival in the port of New York, my total capital consisted of 25 cents.

Even without money, the arrival of the USS Washington in New York harbor was an emotional and unforgettable experience for Fred Rosenfeld. All the passengers were on deck to marvel at the sight of the Statue of Liberty. At first, it made Fred laugh to see his fellow passengers waving their handkerchiefs at a statue. Then someone next to him at the rail explained the meaning of the statue and Fred pulled out his own white handkerchief.

I will never forget my thoughts at that moment. Here I was being welcomed to a strange land, whose language was foreign to me, after being literally thrown out of the country of my birth because I was a Jew. The sight of New York's skyscrapers was awesome. I had never seen such tall buildings in Europe. I was entering a new land full of marvels.

Chapter Four

Cousin Rosa was supposed to meet Fred's ship. Since he was still a minor, someone had to pick him up.

Raised in a small German village, Rosa had been invited to live with the Rosenfeld family in Nuremberg as a teenager. She spent several years as a guest in their apartment before her marriage and immigration to the United States. Since she and her husband were well established in New York, Frieda had written to her, asking her to look after Fred for a while. Rosa had responded immediately, writing back that "after all, you took me in and took care of me when I was young Fred's age. I would be most happy to do the same for you until you can come to the States."

One by one, all of the USS Washington's passengers cleared immigration and departed. Fred was the only one left on board. No one was there to claim him.

Just as I was being told that I would be taken in custody to Ellis Island, Cousin Rosa arrived. I was overjoyed to see her, but she seemed less than happy to see me. She had changed a lot from how I remembered her as a teenager. Her dark hair was swept back like a fashion model, and she walked with her nose pointed up into the air as if she smelled something bad.

Fred and Cousin Rosa left the ship and went by subway to Rosa's home in Jamaica, Queens, New York. They hardly talked on the trip; Rosa seemed irritated at having to speak German and Fred noticed that she smiled and said "good afternoon" in English quite a bit to the strangers they passed.

The first thing Fred did when they got home was to ask Rosa to write on a piece of paper in English: "I am looking for a job." He took this paper with him everywhere he went and wasted no time pounding the sidewalks of New York, going into every store and office with the little piece of paper in hand. On his third day in the city, he landed a job at a small factory on West 49th Street that manufactured expandable metal watch bands. For his salary of six dollars per week, he worked in front of a small press from 8 a.m. to 6 p.m. in a smoky room with forty other workers. Two weeks later, his boss stood behind him, glowering. He had both of his index fingers caught in the press and it was very painful. The boss tapped him on the shoulders and said sarcastically, "I'm so glad we found such a smart boy to work here."

I got angry, so I bandaged my fingers and left that place. A week's pay went down the drain, but my pride was more important to me. Besides, I knew I could find another job in no time.

And he did. Walking down 49th Street, Fred noticed a sign for Zimmerman's Hungarian Restaurant. A rather rotund woman in a yellow dress, with her white hair tied up in a bun, was standing outside the front door. He stopped and struck up a conversation with Mrs. Zimmerman, who spoke German. On the spot, she hired Fred as a porter at twelve dollars per week.

While things were looking up financially, Fred remained miserably homesick and lonely. He was not happy at all living with Cousin Rosa. She and her family treated him like an unwelcome and unwanted guest. Both Rosa and her husband had good jobs and earned what was considered at that time to be good money. They had a relatively spacious apartment with a spare room for Fred, comfortable furniture and a well-stocked cupboard.

As far as I was concerned, they were extremely tight. In fact, many times they would wait until I was in bed before they ate their dinner, so they wouldn't have to feed me. The only reason I stayed with them in the first place was that my mother had written that letter asking her to take care of me until she arrived in about a month. Mother had been careful to assure Rosa that she had enough funds and would reimburse her for whatever she spent on me. And Rosa had answered that she welcomed this opportunity to repay my mother for what she had done in the past for her. My

47

parents had not only kept her for years in our home, but had provided her with a dowry when she got married. Rosa had said that this was her chance to repay a minute part of my parent's generosity, but it certainly didn't work out that way.

On November 9-10, 1938, the infamous *Kristallnacht* took place all over Germany.[4] Thousands of Jews were arrested; their property was confiscated; their synagogues and temples were burned to the ground. Those who wanted to leave after that were told they had to comply with all kinds of new regulations before they could go free. Fred's mother, who had previously been approved for a visa and had booked passage to the U.S. in mid-November, could not leave Germany until late in January 1939.

Soon after receiving the news of Frieda's delay, Fred took the subway to visit another of his cousins, Liesel Vendig, in her New York apartment. He was growing quite familiar with New York's crowded streets and subway stations, and in fact preferred them to the strained atmosphere at Rosa's home. It had been several years since Fred and Liesel had seen each other at one family gathering or another. Liesel was closer to Fred in age, but old enough to have married and immigrated to the U.S. Once teased for being too athletic and a tomboy, she had grown into a tall, attractive woman, with long jet black braids and a rosy glow in her cheeks.

---

[4] The incident was originally referred to as *Kristallnacht* (literally "crystal night"), alluding to the enormous number of glass windows broken throughout the night, mostly in synagogues and Jewish-owned shops.

I walked through the streets to Liesel's address feeling trepidation. Would she be like Rosa? Did life in America turn one inexorably against visiting relatives, negating all the closeness of family we had once enjoyed? I remembered good times with Liesel even when we boys had teased her. She had been a good sport about it, but maybe now that I was at a disadvantage, she would hold it against me.

When Fred entered Liesel's apartment, he saw right away that she had been crying.

"What's the matter, Liesel?"

"You have to leave Rosa's house at once and come to live with me," she answered.

Fred was perplexed. "What has happened?"

At first, she was reluctant to answer, but finally she admitted that Rosa had come to visit her that day. "She told me her home was not a welfare institution," Liesel said with a sneer. "I was enraged! How can you say this, I asked her, after all Aunt Frieda and Uncle Leopold did for you? She had no answer for me so I asked her to leave my home and never come back. I was disgusted by her behavior. You cannot live with them, Fred. Go get your things immediately."

I was relieved and saddened. I couldn't understand what had happened to make Rosa think the way she did. I went to her apartment and gathered my things without saying a word. As the door closed behind me, I thought, tonight they'll be able to eat their dinner at a decent hour!

Fred's new home was a one-bedroom apartment in Manhattan. Closer to his work, it was still awkward, with Fred sleeping on a small couch in the tiny living room. It wasn't long before his cousin Leo and his wife Bertha found out about Fred's predicament and invited him to stay in their large flat. And so, he spent the holidays with Bertha and Leo, waiting for his mother and Uncle to arrive. When their ship arrived, Fred met them at the pier and handed his mother 60 one-dollar bills, the money he had saved thus far.

Chapter Five

Uncle Max, Frieda and Fred moved into a two-bedroom apartment on Wadsworth Terrace not far from Bertha and Leo. Liesel too was right in the neighborhood, and so they all resumed the closeness they had once enjoyed in Germany. For Fred it was a very happy time. Three years since he had last lived with his mother, he had been given a chance to make up for lost time. Most important, she and Uncle Max had escaped the horrors of 1939 Germany. Only Uncle Siegfried remained, and he was booked on a ship leaving Le Havre.

One day Frieda asked Fred to show her the restaurant where he worked. She wanted to know how her son made such a living. Fred went to work each morning before the sun was up, so Frieda came on her own later in the morning. Having learned the subway system quickly, she had no trouble finding her way to Zimmerman's Hungarian Restaurant on 49th Street. Turning the corner, she saw her only son polishing the brass doors to the restaurant and nearly started to cry.

"Fred, stop," she said. "Come home with me. You don't have to do this kind of work. I have some money. You can find something easier than this."

Fred laid down his polishing rag and took Frieda by the shoulders. "No, mother," he said. "I've taken enough money from you. Now I'm on my own."

"But Fred," she said. "You worked so hard in school. You wanted to be an engineer. Look at what you're doing."

"Believe me, mother, this is just a way of getting started. You'll see."

That year, 1939, the World's Fair took place in New York, and it was the talk of the town. Everyone went to see it. On one of his days off, Fred invited Frieda to be his guest for the day at the fair. They left early and reached the fairgrounds as the gates opened. It was a warm and sunny day, following a rainy night so that early on steam rose off the streets. They meandered from pavilion to pavilion, marveling at displays from distant lands — China, Egypt, Brazil. Fred told his mother that someday they would travel to such places, and she laughed.

The Italian pavilion was reputed to be the nicest. Fred led Frieda there at lunchtime because it was widely known that on top was the best restaurant of the fair. He was anxious to treat her to a good meal. At the entrance, they stopped to read the posted menu and Frieda saw Fred's color change when he noted the prices.

"Let's go in," she said. "It will be my treat."

Fred shook his head. "No way," he said. "I invited you.

I'll pay, but we'll go someplace else to eat. The food here can't be that good."

As we were about to leave, I noticed a sign — Help Wanted, Apply Restaurant Office. I asked my mother to have a seat on a bench nearby, telling her I'd be right back. Then I was off to the restaurant office, combing my hair back with my fingers and making sure my shirt was tucked into my pants. There was a line of men and women waiting to be interviewed. I was soon third in line and I could hear one man ahead of me being questioned: "What do you do?"

"I'm a bartender." he answered.

"Do you speak Italian?" The answer was no. "Sorry, we need only cooks and waiters." The next man was about to be interviewed. "What's your name?" It was Smith or something like that. "Sorry, we're only hiring Italians."

I was next. "Your name?"

"Alfredo Rossi" was my answer, spoken in my best Italian accent.

"What do you do?"

"I'm a waiter."

"Where have you worked?"

I quickly named two hotels where my mother and I had stayed at different times in Milan. The man was satisfied and I was hired on the spot to start the next day. My pay would come from the service charges added to each bill, a common practice in European restaurants.

Later that evening, when Fred finally told Frieda and

Uncle Max how he had landed his new job, they were outraged.

"How could you do a thing like this? It's illegal!" shouted Uncle Max.

"It's not illegal."

"It's immoral, then. You'll end up in jail when they find out. You've never been a waiter in your life. You know nothing about the job, and what's worse, you used a false name!"

Fred had been in America a little longer than Frieda and Max, and he shrugged off their concerns. "I can do this job. If they find out, the only thing they can do is fire me."

I went back to Zimmerman's that night and told them that I'd found a better job that started the next day. They tried to get me to stay. Mrs. Zimmerman even offered me a two dollar per week raise, but I suspected that at the Italian restaurant I would make much more. My hours were from 10:30 a.m. until three in the afternoon, and then again from five p.m. until closing, which was normally about one a.m., but many times as late as three. The train took well over an hour to get to and from work, which meant I got very little sleep.

But Fred was still young enough not to need much sleep, and he made lots of money. One night, when he came home around four a.m., Uncle Max awoke at the sound of the door closing. Fred held up his first paycheck for $55 for his uncle to see. Without the light on, Max squinted at it and said, "Twenty-five dollars! Very good."

Fred shook his head, "It's $55, Uncle Max. Fifty-five

dollars for one week's work!"

Fred had assured him so loudly that Frieda woke up and came into the room.

"What's all this fuss about?" she asked.

Fred showed the check. "And that's not all I made this week," he said, grinning. "Americans aren't familiar with the system of adding a service charge to the bill, so most of them leave me a tip anyway. With all that cash, I made nearly one hundred dollars this week!"

I could see that my mother and Uncle Max were still worried about the whole affair, but the truth was they had nothing to worry about. Of course my first day on that job was a real experience and I nearly got found out for having never waited on tables before. I was assigned a station. My boss Pietro, the maitre d' hotel, *took the orders; I delivered them. When I presented myself to him, he said, "Go ahead and set the tables. The busboys will help you."*

I had never done anything like this before, not even at home. So, I went slowly, watching what the others did and following suit. As the customers arrived, one ordered wine with his meal and Pietro told me to go get white wine glasses. I knew what a glass looks like, but I had never seen so many glasses in my entire life — there were red wine glasses, white wine glasses, champagne glasses, liquor glasses, water glasses, cocktail glasses, cognac glasses and God only knows what other glasses. I had no idea what I was looking for. To me, at that stage in my life, a glass was a glass no matter what you put in it. So, I stood there wondering.

A dishwasher passed by and I said to him, "Where the hell did you put the white wine glasses?" He said, "Right there, right in front of your nose," pointing to the glasses I needed. That's how I overcame my first crisis as a waiter.

Pietro was from Milan. Before long, Fred befriended him and even confessed that he had fibbed a little to get the job. He told him that he had exaggerated his experience by saying he had worked in big fancy hotels, when in fact, he had only worked in small simple places. It was still a lie, but told in the Milan dialect of which Fred was quite proficient and Pietro was quite proud. It did the trick.

"I'd be very grateful to you, if you would correct me when I do anything wrong," Fred asked him.

"Of course, of course my friend," Pietro agreed. "We are like brothers and I will help you with pleasure."

Fred's multi-national form of luck was only beginning to reveal itself. Pietro took him under his wing and grew fonder and fonder of him, in contrast to the other waiters who came mostly from the south of Italy. Together they formed the only niche of typical Milanese culture at the restaurant.

As the war in Europe progressed, however, the Italian restaurant became less and less popular. All of the employees who were hired in the United States were laid off. Most of the restaurant workers came from two Italian luxury liners — *Conte di Savoy* and *Rex* — that went back and forth between the United States and Italy. In fact, the restaurant was owned and operated by the Italian-American Steamship Line.

It looked like the end of my career as a waiter after less than six weeks. I rested at home for a few days, until a mailman came to our door asking if someone by the name of Alfredo Rossi lived in this apartment. He had a special delivery letter from Pietro, asking me to come back for an interview. When I got there, I found out that I was the only one they had asked to come back because I worked hard, but mostly because of my friendship with Pietro.

"Do you own a white dinner jacket," Pietro asked Fred.

Fred did. Just before leaving Italy, he had a white silk jacket made to order and had never worn it.

"We don't need you as a waiter. You will be in charge of taking reservations and assigning tables."

At first Fred worried that the job would mean a cut in pay since he didn't think he would collect the lucrative extra tips. But it turned out to be an even better job. Fred soon learned that big tips were the norm from customers who were seated at good tables with a view. He also learned how to spot the big tippers and before long was making nearly double his previous salary.

One day the King George VI and Queen Elizabeth of England came to the World's Fair. Fred was at his post near the front door of the restaurant when one of the bosses came around passing out fascist insignias for all of the restaurant's employees to wear.

"What the hell is this?" he asked.

"We want to send a message to the British royalty," was the man's reply. "When they come by tomorrow morning, we want everyone lined up in front of the pavilion to boo them."

I made up my mind right then and there not to be a part of this. There was no question. I refused even to touch that insignia and walked out the front door of the restaurant, leaving the boss with his jaw hanging.

Chapter Six

By this time, Fred had saved a little nest egg by putting half of his tips and half of his regular pay into an interest-bearing bank account. He was quite proud of that money and thought he was ready to go into business for himself. The only question was, doing what?

Frieda heard him talking about it at the breakfast table one morning and despite her better judgment decided to tell him about a distant relative, Mannfried Gerstein, who had recently arrived in New York from Germany. He was related to Uncle David by marriage and back home he had owned and operated a leather business.

"He hasn't learned to speak English yet," said Frieda. "And if I know him, he probably won't do it anytime soon. Plus, he doesn't have any money thanks to Hitler. But I know he had a good business over there and he wants to get back into business here. Why don't you talk to him?"

Fred didn't need any prodding. Leather sounded like as good a business as any. After all, everybody wore leather shoes. He met Mannfried at the older man's tiny Bronx apartment. Mannfried was in his early forties, tall and handsome, with dark, wavy hair and bushy eyebrows that gave him a thoughtful look. They hit it off at once and soon hammered out a fifty-fifty agreement — Mannfried would do the buying, Fred would do the selling.

Even then with as little business experience as I had, I knew the importance of the buying process, since that was where a lot of the profit would be made. The first day, he went out with the money I gave him and bought a 100-pound bag of shoe leather, soles only. We sorted it all at Mannfried's place by size and quality. He taught me the difference between a good piece of leather and a not-so-good piece. Then we packaged them into dozen-pair bundles. After our first day of work, Mannfried insisted we buy a bottle of brandy and toast to our success.

Fred began his new career, calling on shoemakers throughout Manhattan. His policy was to persuade them to try some of his leather at no initial cost, and then return in a week to see if they were willing to pay the price and buy more. Since Mannfried knew his leather well and purchased a high grade, all the shoemakers seemed pleased. Just as important, however, was the rapport that Fred developed with them. They were mostly Italians; shoemaking was and still is to some extent an Italian calling. And, once again, Fred used his Italian language skills to his best advantage.

Business got better and better for M&F Leather. Before too long, the partners hired a pretty young Mexican girl named Maria to keep the books and rented an office and warehouse in the leather district of lower Manhattan.

At that stage, I was on the road sometimes for as long as five weeks at a time. I bought a '36 Ford for $160 and traveled from upstate New York to Washington D.C., staying in two-dollar-a-night hotels and eating five-cent frankfurters or ten-cent hamburgers in order to have more funds available for my partner to buy leather.

After many marathon road trips, Fred returned to New York one afternoon in late November. An early winter storm had just passed through the city, leaving two inches of slush and snow on the streets and sidewalks. Fred arrived at the office before five, found the door locked and opened it with his key.

The place was empty — no leather, no partner, no secretary either. I checked the only thing left to check, all the records neatly filed by Maria in a tall metal file cabinet behind her desk. I immediately noticed that some of my first and best customers, the Italian shoemakers of Manhattan and the surrounding boroughs, had not paid their bills in some time.

Fred spent the rest of that day and into that night visiting his old friends in their tiny shops and stores. One by one, he asked them if they had been having problems with

M&F. One by one, they assured him there were no problems.

"Why do you ask?"

"I noticed that our latest shipments have not been paid." Fred held the unpaid invoices up as proof.

The shoemakers insisted they had paid and dug out canceled checks or cash receipts as their proof.

That was the bleak end to my leather business. Mannfried Gerstein completely disappeared with all the money, and, as I later found out, with pretty young Maria. The two of them, it seems, decided to find a better life in Mexico.

Shortly after Fred left his World's Fair job, Uncle Siegfried had arrived in the United States, the last member of Fred's immediate family to escape from Germany. During the summer of 1940, Frieda, Max and Siegfried purchased a chicken farm in Vineland, New Jersey.

Fred stayed behind in a small rented room in the city. He was on the road so often; he was seldom there. The morning after the demise of what had been a very successful leather business, Fred drove the Ford to Vineland.

Frieda shook her head at the news of Mannfried's disappearance. She wanted to kick herself for not anticipating it. In Germany, Mannfried had had a reputation as a ladies' man and fickle character prone to impulsive behavior. But his business had always done well.

"You should continue with the business," she told Fred. "I can give you money. Let me finance you."

"No. I won't take any more of your money," Fred said.

"It's bad enough that I lost my own money. I'm in no mood to take yours and maybe lose it too."

Uncle Max scoffed at this. "You won't lose any more money, if I know my boy Fred," he said. "You always did learn your lesson."

But Fred would not listen. His only concession was to move into a spare room on the farm and begin the search for a new job. One thing he knew for certain was that he would not work with the chickens.

On December 7, 1941, Fred packed up his things in his Manhattan room and made the move to New Jersey. Driving down the Westside Highway to the Holland Tunnel, he was listening to a football game on the radio. Suddenly the broadcast was interrupted by a news bulletin: Japanese aircraft had bombed Pearl Harbor.

> *I was shocked. Everyone was shocked. Cars were pulling off the highway, people getting out, shaking their heads in horror. I pulled over too, got out and leaned against the car door. From the shoulder of the highway I could look out across the river at the shore of New Jersey. To the north sunlight glinted off cars crossing the George Washington Bridge as the radio announcer continued to describe the surprise attack.*

Fred proceeded into New Jersey and was stopped near the state line by a police roadblock. "Where are you headed, sir?" asked a tall state trooper, wearing dark sunglasses. It turned out that servicemen had been recalled to their posts and they were looking for rides. Fred agreed to carry three soldiers to Fort Dix. One of them had just left Fort Dix that morning and was on his way home to Albany on his first furlough. He never made it. As Fred's car sped south on I-95, the four young men inside listened intently to the radio. All regular programs had been suspended, and even the football game had been stopped. News messages and marching music were the order of the day.

One evening just a few days later, Fred and his family sat in the living room of their Vineland home, listening to the radio. About nine o'clock, they heard a new song by Sammy Kaye: "Remember Pearl Harbor."

During those days, the country had an air of patriotism as I had never seen before or since. Everyone wanted to help their country. War was officially declared, first with the Japanese, and shortly after with the Germans and Italians. Because I was 100 percent broke, I took the first job that came my way. It was in a clothing factory in Vineland, making army overcoats. My job was to cut collars all day. I didn't find this to be too exciting, so I was looking for something better.

In January, Fred answered an advertisement in the local paper and took a job as timekeeper at Seabrook Farms, one of the country's largest food packagers, specializing in frozen vegetables for the government and for national brands like Birdseye. Fred's job was to compute wages for workers on all the production lines. It was much better than doing piecework because it gave him the freedom to move around the plant. He even spent time in the executive offices. As a result, he quickly became very friendly with the CEO's secretary, Betty Maldonado, a pretty woman about ten years older than Fred. One day, as they ate lunch together, she told Fred that the company was getting ready to go into dehydration of vegetables for export to the allies as well as for the troops going overseas.

"They're talking about finding some bright guy to send to school on dehydration so we can have at least one so-called expert on the process," Betty said, as she munched on a carrot stick. "They say it's going to be the wave of the future and somebody around here better know what they're doing."

Fred went home that night and wrote letters to every food magazine and university he could think of to get articles and information on food dehydration. Less than a week later, he received several brochures and a book from the local university. It seemed to contain everything he needed to know about the most modern methods of food dehydration in simple language. Fred read it cover to cover in one night.

Another week went by, and Fred was called in to see Mr. Tomkins, the business manager.

"We're going to need to make some changes to our timekeeping system, Fred," Mr. Tomkins said.

"Whatever you need sir, we can do it and do it quickly," Fred replied. "If you don't mind my asking though, what are these changes all about?"

Mr. Tomkins went to his window and pointed to a new building under construction at the far end of the Seabrook property. "You see that building there, Fred? Well, it's the future being built right before our eyes. It's going to be home to Seabrook's new dehydration operation. We'll need to develop a timekeeping system for the new workers."

"Dehydration, huh? That's been a fascination of mine for some time. I've studied quite a bit about that."

Mr. Tomkins raised his eyebrows. He seemed very impressed. "We need to discuss this further," he said. "I'll set up a meeting with J.B."

Fred's heart was pounding as he jogged back to his office. J.B. was Betty's boss, the company's CEO. That same afternoon, Fred was ushered into his office, where Mr. Tomkins was waiting for him with J.B., Seabrook's president, Nathan Summerville, the company's sales manager and the chief engineer.

J.B. wasted no time getting to the point. "We understand you know quite a bit about dehydration, Fred."

"I've studied it," Fred agreed. "To be honest with you, I've been approached recently by several companies who are going into dehydration. Some of them have even made me offers, but I really don't want to relocate. My family is here and all that."

The look on their faces almost made me laugh out loud. Now the real questions started and the main interrogator was the chief engineer, who obviously got his questions out of the same book from which I got the answers. After about a half hour, I was excused. When I passed Betty on my way out, she winked at me.

Fred was cleaning up his desk, getting ready to go home, when the phone rang. It was Betty. "He wants to see you again, right away," she said.

This time Fred was alone with J.B.

"I want to send you to Rutgers for a course on dehydration," J.B. said. "Then you'll go to Washington and take a two-week course offered by the War Production Board. We'll maintain your full salary, of course, during the time you're in school. And all your expenses will be paid. After you graduate, you'll step into a very high position in our dehydration department. How's that sound, Fred?"

Fred smiled and said, "To be honest with you, sir, I've had some far better offers from some of our competitors. But, I would stay here, if..."

J.B. leaned across his big mahogany desk and looked Fred right in the eyes. "What are your conditions?"

I took a moment to gather my thoughts and then I let him have it. "First, I'd like a raise from $25 to $35 a week. You pay all my expenses while I'm in school and when I graduate, I want another raise to $50. If I complete the courses satisfactorily, which I assure you I will, I want to be in charge of the dehydration department."

J.B. sat back in his chair and ran his hand over his thin grey hair. "You drive a hard bargain. I'll have to discuss this with others, Fred. But if I were you, I'd start packing for Rutgers."

The following Friday, J.B. personally handed Fred his

first $35. "You report to Rutgers on Monday morning, Fred. We have all the confidence in the world in you. You'll get everything you asked for if you complete both courses successfully. I'll be personally checking on your progress."

Chapter Seven

I took and completed both courses within three months'
time, and I knew as much before the courses as I did after I
finished. They were a complete waste of time. It was all
theory and as new to the school as it was to everyone else.
I'm not complaining, mind you. For a little while I felt like
a real Ivy League college Joe. I met some very pretty coeds on
campus and lived the carefree life of a subsidized student,
while many boys my age were already facing the horrors of
World War II.

When Fred returned to Seabrook Farms, he was
immediately named to the post of manager of the dehydration
department. The new building was ready but empty, and for a
few days Fred worked alone in his office, listening to the silence
of the great hall outside. Then the dehydration equipment
arrived in giant wooden crates and along with them came an
engineer from the factory to install it all.

Tom Crocker, the engineer, asked me where I wanted to place each machine for maximum efficiency. I had no idea, so I asked for his advice. In fact, I let him set the stuff up wherever he wanted, knowing that his company was the only manufacturer of this equipment and he had done this before.

Testing began. Fred and his small staff spent long hours running vegetables through the machines. They ruined most of what they tried before everything was running smoothly. Fortunately, they spent that entire week without any interference from the company's top brass. J.B. was in Washington D.C. with his executive team, trying to get government orders. On the following Monday, word came to prepare to demonstrate the dehydration of beets and potatoes for U.S. Army representatives on Thursday morning at eight o'clock sharp.

"We're in deep shit," Fred said, late on Tuesday night in his office. Across the desk, Tom Crocker looked amused.

"What are you worrying about, everything is running fine now."

"I'm not so sure. Every other batch of beets still comes out black. We can't have any screw-ups during the demonstration."

"We've got a whole day tomorrow to practice," said Tom. "Tomorrow night you can worry if we haven't got it down."

By the next night, they had perfected the process, at least

for beets and potatoes. Fred slept well on the eve of the demonstration. All day Thursday, the Army representatives marveled at the clean new machinery, in a building that still smelled of fresh pine wood. Fred showed them how bushels of beets and potatoes could be quickly reduced to small, easy to transport quantities. For lunch, they dined at a picnic table outside Fred's office on the same beets and potatoes, cooked by Tom Crocker on a stovetop in the back room.

Seabrook landed a huge order. On Friday morning, Fred was called to J.B.'s office to discuss production,

"How much can you produce in an eight-hour shift?" J.B. asked.

Fred shifted on his feet, smoothed his hair back and studied the ceiling as if the answer might be written there. "It depends," he hedged.

"I need to know exactly," J.B. said. "The same for a 16-hour shift and a 24-hour shift."

I figured I could get a bonus if I produced more than what I said I could, so I sat down and did some calculations on paper. I handed J.B. three figures that I felt very comfortable with, that I was certain we could produce with no problems. Just as I expected, J.B circled the 24-hour shift figure and he told me that he would pay me a bonus for anything over that.

"In fact, Fred my boy, this is so big that I'll increase your salary if you can produce 10 percent more than that."

Fred beamed.

"But let me tell you," J.B. continued. "Now is the time to put up or shut up."

At that moment, I was overcome with the thought that I had faked my way to this point. I really didn't know a lot about what I was supposed to do. Tom Crocker was the real expert, and he was at that very moment on a train back to his own company in Pennsylvania. I was alone, and if I failed, I would be out as a manager, out as a timekeeper and probably couldn't get a job at Seabrook as an office boy. I had to make it go.

Fred hired eleven workers and set up three shifts running around the clock. He was working 18 to 20 hours a day, falling asleep for a few hours in his car with the sound of the dehydration plant still humming in the background. The car's trunk always held a fresh change of clothes. Fred took showers in the men's restroom and ate in the company cafeteria. Every three days, he drove home to Vineland for one of Frieda's meals and more clothes.

It worked. Fred's team produced 26 percent more than he had estimated. True to his word, J.B. gave him a substantial raise. By the spring of 1942, Fred was making more money than ever before.

There was only one problem. The chief engineer, who had questioned Fred about dehydration in J.B.'s office several months before, had been assigned to manage one of the daytime shifts. He was about 50 years old and took no pleasure in having a 22-year-old boss. At every opportunity, the man made comments about how terrible it was to see healthy young men around town while his own son, who had been married just two months before, was on his way to fight the Japanese.

"Of course, I don't mean you, Fred," he was always quick to add. "You're doing important government work."

Hearing the same speech every day had a strange effect on Fred. As busy as he was, he didn't hear much about the war effort. But now, he took notice of the fact that a majority of his co-workers were older men because the younger ones had dropped out of the workforce to join one branch or another of the Armed Services. He listened to Frieda, Uncle Max and Siegfried around the dinner table sadly discussing the state of affairs back home in Germany. Their friends and relatives were trapped in the grip of something no one here in America could fully comprehend yet.

Naturally, I felt guilty. But I was growing angry too. Maybe I was beginning to feel my oats, so to speak. Maybe I could have a turn at trying to fix a world gone haywire. In all the time I had spent here in America, my only thought had been how to take advantage of the world of opportunity thrown into my lap. It had all come so easily. I had forgotten about being thrown down the steps of the soccer stadium by Streicher's goon squad.

Fred's first army deferment because of his work expired on June 10, 1942. The next morning, he skipped work and reported for duty at the Vineland Army recruiting office. A sergeant swore him in at 8:15 a.m., and by nine o'clock, Fred was at J.B.'s office.

"He's in Washington, Fred, getting you more big orders," Betty Maldonado told him.

"I'll just leave him a note," Fred said.

Betty took the note when Fred was finished scribbling it and read it out loud: "I hereby inform you that I will be out of the office for the remainder of the hunting season. Thanks for everything."

Betty frowned. "What's this supposed to mean?"

"I'm going to war," Fred told her. "Make sure he gets that, will you?"

The next day J.B. called Fred at home. "You can't do this, Fred. You're exempt from active duty because you're doing war work. I'm calling them to get you out."

He hung up before Fred could protest.

Fred continued to pack his things. Seabrook didn't really need him and he knew somehow that his days there were over. When J.B. called back an hour later, he told Fred that since he was already sworn in, there was nothing anyone could do.

One week later, Fred reported for active duty at Fort Dix in New Jersey.

Chapter Eight

Fred's cousin, Rudy Mannheimer, lived in Vineland at the time, working as a toolmaker in one of the large local factories. For months he had tried to enlist.

"If anyone has a reason to fight the Germans, it's us," he would say to Fred. "Those bastards took away everything we had, our homes and even our country. If it weren't for the grace of God, our families would not be in America."

Rudy had tried the Navy, the Coast Guard and even the Merchant Marines. Throughout 1941, he was turned down again and again as an enemy alien. But by 1942, with the war escalating on two distant fronts, the United States had relaxed its enlistment criteria. Both Fred and Rudy received draft notices. While Fred went into the Army, Rudy opted for the Navy.

Arriving at Fort Dix (near Trenton, New Jersey) to be inducted was quite an experience for me. Our bus was met by a soldier with one stripe on his arm, making him a private first class. He treated us like a herd of cattle. But he was a veteran with 20 years of service, and our commander, so we had to follow his orders. He drove us through all the induction procedures and then to our barracks, where he assigned each of us a bunk.

In the quartermaster supply building, Fred and his new mates were issued everything from sheets to underwear, shoes and leggings. The U.S. Army, however, did not possess a uniform that would fit someone as short and skinny as poor Fred. He spent the next two days at Fort Dix clothed only in long underwear, and since this was not proper soldier's attire, he was assigned to kitchen duty until they could find him a uniform that fit.

In the kitchen, Fred learned a tidbit of Army information — how many potatoes would fit into a 55-gallon drum and how long it took to peel that many.

Finally, my uniform arrived, like a graduation present from the mess hall. Then the induction process resumed. I was interviewed several times to find out just where I fit into the organization. It began to look like I would be assigned to the ski troops and transferred to Camp Carson in Colorado as a ski instructor. I was, after all, quite a proficient skier since the age of four. As a student in Italy, I had even won a number of tournaments, not to mention the many hours I spent with young Italian girls on the slopes of the Alps.

Then something strange happened. Fred was brought before a board of six men, three in civilian dress and three in officers' uniforms. The first thing they asked him was whether he would have any trouble with the idea of fighting Germans. "You are still essentially a German citizen," commented one of the civilians.

"I probably want to fight them more than you do," Fred replied. "They attacked my family and my religion. I have no scruples about fighting them. In fact, given the choice, that's exactly where I would most prefer to fight."

They all seemed pleased with this response. For a moment they conferred among themselves, and all Fred could hear was unintelligible murmuring. Then, an officer stepped forward and escorted Fred outside the room. "We'll only be a minute," he said, slipping back inside.

Ten minutes passed. When they called Fred back in, one of the men in civilian clothes said, "We need you for a very special top secret assignment."

Fred nodded.

"You'll have to volunteer," the man continued, "but, unfortunately, we can't tell you any further details about what the assignment will entail. You'll learn that in due course."

At that moment, I suddenly remembered the instructions we had received from the private first class who had inducted us at Fort Dix. He had said, "The best way to get along in this Army is to keep your eyes open and your mouth shut. Never volunteer."

Fred was certain this advice was meant for just such an occasion. "I'm sorry," he said, "but if you can't tell me more, I can't volunteer."

The group no longer looked so pleased. They sent him back to the barracks, and the very next morning Fred and his platoon were shipped to infantry training at Camp Croft, South Carolina. For the next two weeks, they learned to march, salute, pack a field pack and all the other essentials of good soldiering.

Early one morning, Fred was called to camp headquarters, and found himself facing another collection of men in and out of uniform. They asked more or less the same questions and ended with the same statement: "We want you to volunteer for a top secret assignment we can't tell you anything more about."

Fred's answer was the same, "If I don't know what it is, I can't volunteer."

A few days went by and the platoon was shipped to Camp Shenango, Pennsylvania. On the way, the talk was all about finally getting to learn how to use a gun. Everyone was anxious for that, but up to then there had been no indication that the Army would ever provide such training.

The troop train arrived at the camp depot in the dead of night. At that hour, the young recruits could see little difference between Shenango and the other army camps they had experienced in their short careers. In the morning, they learned the difference.

This was the most miserable place of my Army career. It had

78

*been an Army penal camp and was turned into a port of
embarkation just before we got there. Our group was the
first to be assigned there, and apparently not all of the
criminals had left yet. The real problem was that the Army
had failed to change the camp personnel. Prison guards were
taking care of us, the new recruits. It was a tough place.
Officers, enlisted men, even chaplains were prone to go
AWOL from Camp Shenango.*

Contrary to their hope of learning to shoot rifles, no
training was scheduled at the camp. The new recruits were
there to wait and nothing more. It was to be their port of
embarkation to the war. One day they were issued winter
uniforms, the next day summer uniforms. One day they were
told that they would be going to England, the next it was
Africa.

Finally, they were assigned to a company that was part of
the First Infantry Division and issued rifles and bayonets in
preparation for going overseas.

*I took the rifle they gave me, but I had no idea how it
worked, no one did. When we asked about training, we
were told, "You'll get on-the-job training in due time."*

The group was informed that, since they would be going
overseas soon, their relatives would be allowed to visit Camp
Shenango. Each soldier was given a 24-hour pass. Fred called
his mother and told her where he was. "You should come to
visit," he said. "It isn't too far a drive from Vineland."

They came in Uncle Max's car on a Saturday. Fred met them at the gate, not wanting them to see the conditions of the camp. They took a drive through the Pennsylvania countryside, stopped for lunch at a roadside dinner and talked mainly about family gossip. The chicken farm was prospering. "You should come home and work with us," Max told Fred. "Why bother with this Army stuff?"

The cousins were still living in Manhattan. Frieda visited all of them regularly, including Rosa. Rudy was somewhere in New England, training to be a Navy seaman. "His mother is sick about it," said Frieda, shaking her head. "Look what happened to all those Navy boys at Pearl Harbor."

Eventually, the conversation turned to Fred's future.

"Oh, I'll be going through training for some time," Fred lied, not wanting them to know how soon the army planned to send him overseas. They said good-bye at the Camp Shenango gate. Fred stood there waving and watched Uncle Max's car until it was out of sight.

Several days later, he was called again before a collection of men in and out of uniform. This time, they told him much the same about the secret assignment with one very important difference. "This assignment will require you to go through extensive training."

I had heard the magic word — training. Considering my situation, waiting at Camp Shenango to go overseas with a fully trained infantry division and still not even knowing how to clean my gun, I signed up for the secret assignment immediately. The men in the room nodded and smiled at me, and I felt like some kind of a guinea pig about to undergo a dangerous experiment. One of the officers told me to go back to my quarters and await further orders.

In the middle of the next night, Fred's division received orders to take its equipment, including tropical uniforms, and assemble in front of the barracks. From there, they were marched to a special train that was waiting to take them to a ship, destination still unknown.

As I sat on the train with my duffel bag and all my belongings, my heart was sinking. I figured I had waited too long to sign up for the extra training and the top secret job. Instead, I would soon find myself in the middle of some godforsaken battle, wondering how to load my gun.

Suddenly, Fred heard a voice calling out his name. It was a lieutenant, rushing through the train looking for him. When he located Fred, he said, "Get off the train, Rosenfeld. You're not leaving. Go back to your barracks and report to post intelligence first thing tomorrow morning."

Fred tossed his duffel bag out the window and jumped off the train. He hadn't been on the platform more than a minute before the train pulled out. Later, he would learn that the division had been sent to North Africa, where it sustained tremendous losses battling Rommel's tank forces in the Algerian desert.

I slept well that night all alone in the barracks while my former mates began their long journey to the war. In the unusual quiet, without the sounds of three dozen snoring, coughing, sleep-talking men, I felt lucky, perhaps even blessed. It wasn't that I didn't want to fight. On the contrary, I was determined to face the enemy. I just didn't want to do it without knowing how.

Chapter Nine

The next morning, Fred reported to the post intelligence officer as ordered. Colonel Miller was a tall, dark-haired man just beginning to grow grey at the temples. He seldom smiled and spoke in a hushed, gravelly voice like a man with a bad sore throat.

"Welcome to the Army's police force," he said. "Your first assignment will be right here at Camp Shenango. You've been here awhile so I assume you know the problems we face. The old cadre hasn't been replaced fast enough, so we're dealing with a prison camp mentality."

Fred nodded.

"But there are plenty of other problems brewing. Most of these boys are scared shitless and they have nothing to do but wait to be shipped out. Drug abuse is on the rise, and racial tensions are running high. Are you prepared to deal with some ugly situations?"

Fred nodded, beginning to realize what his new job would be like. During his brief stay at Camp Shenango, he had seen fights erupt and smelled the unmistakable odor of marijuana smoke, but he had made it a point to steer clear of such behavior. Now, he would be thrust into the middle of it.

"I've seen little guys like you turn out to be pretty tough customers," Colonel Miller continued. "Think you can handle yourself?"

"Yes sir," Fred said.

"Good."

He was given a Military Police band for his uniform and a nightstick to carry at all times. His new mates were all much bigger than him, but no one questioned his ability to hold his own. Two days into the assignment, Camp Shenango had its biggest race riot ever when a drug deal went sour. Fred was off duty, reading a book in his bunk. He heard the shouting, grabbed his stick and raced into the night. Before he knew it, he was in the middle of a free-for-all.

It was the first time in his life that Fred hit another human being. He tried not to at first, but shouting at the brawling soldiers was pointless. When he tried to pull two fighters apart, someone slugged him in the mouth and somebody else jumped on his back. Fred was stunned by the sudden pain and the metallic taste of blood in his mouth. He fell to his knees and felt the air being choked out of him from behind. On instinct, Fred lashed out with the nightstick and heard a sickening crack as it hit its mark. The hands around his neck loosened and let go.

It seemed like hours before Camp Shenango was quiet

again. That night Fred nursed a split lip, two black eyes and an ugly red welt that started below his left ear and traveled across his face and down his neck. During the next several days, sporadic fighting broke out throughout the camp. With each encounter, Fred grew more brazen in his defense of peace and quiet.

After several weeks of this, Colonel Miller called me to his office. I must have looked like a prizefighter with my slowly healing scars and faded black eyes. I think I saw the Colonel actually grin for a moment.

"Congratulations, Rosenfeld," Colonel Miller said, handing Fred his orders in a brown Manila envelope. "You're going to the military intelligence training center at Fort Ritchie, Maryland."

Fred had developed a suspicious nature since joining the military police. He eyed the envelope warily and said nothing.

"Fort Ritchie is just outside Washington, D.C.," the Colonel added. "You won't have to worry about keeping order there. It's time for your training. They'll turn you into a top-notch intelligence officer there." Fred was to become one of the Ritchie Boys, a special military intelligence unit comprised mainly of German-speaking U.S. immigrants. They were predominantly Jews, most of whom like Fred had fled Nazi persecution, utilized for interrogation of prisoners on the front lines and counter-intelligence in Europe because of their knowledge of the German language and culture.

Fort Ritchie was a beautiful place, very much the opposite of Camp Shenango. Set among pleasant country surroundings, it was close enough to the nation's capital to make Saturday night leave more fun. I didn't always take off on leave, though, because the camp food was excellent. It was prepared by Italian prisoners of war.

Fred began taking courses. It was a far cry from his days at Rutgers studying food dehydration. His first classes were Interrogation of Prisoners of War, Italian and German; Order of Battle; German Geography and Psychology; and Propaganda. He studied harder than ever before, knowing that these courses could mean the difference between life and death someday very soon.

In September, Fred's group was sent to Fort Leonard Wood, Missouri to train with the 75th Infantry Division. They hadn't been on maneuvers long enough to start complaining about the mosquitoes before a message came from Washington to return to Ritchie at once to prepare for overseas transfer. They boarded a train on September 8, 1942.

The sun was setting on a perfect Indian summer day. An orange glow suffused the railroad car. One group of soldiers played cards near the front of the car, others read or napped in their seats. Fred was lost in a reverie, when Lieutenant Morgan, one of his commanding officers, sat down across the aisle.

"How ya doin', Fred? Everything goin' OK?"

Fred smiled. "Everything's looking rosy," he replied.

"Listen, Fred, I've been thinkin' about us heading overseas soon. I've been thinkin' about you in particular."

"About me?"

"Yeah, Fred, I've been thinkin' about your name, your last name that is – Rosenfeld. That's a very Jewish sounding name."

"Well it should be," Fred shot back, beginning to feel uncomfortable. "I'm as Jewish as I can be."

"Now, I know that Fred, don't get me wrong. I got nothin' against Jews, but Hitler sure as hell does. I just think you should consider changing your name to somethin' less German-Jewish sounding. You know, somethin' like Rogers or Roberts. It's going to be hot enough for you over there."

Fred shifted around in his seat. He tried to smile but it turned out looking more like a scowl. The lieutenant stood up.

"Just food for thought, eh, Fred? I didn't mean anything by it."

At first I resisted the idea. But it kept creeping back into my mind. I wasn't mad at Morgan or anything, I just couldn't believe being Jewish had become such a liability. Like they say now, I was still in denial.

When the train stopped for 20 minutes in St. Louis, I wandered through the cavernous Union Station and stopped at a telephone booth. Inside a tattered telephone directory hung from a chain. I opened it and turned the pages to the RO section. Then I closed my eyes and ran my finger down the page. When I stopped and opened my eyes, I saw the name Rodell for the first time. I was 23 years old, and my name was now Fred Rodell.

Back at Fort Ritchie, Fred wrote to his mother: "On the advice of one of my officers, I've decided to change my name. I hope you won't mind, Mother, but they tell me I'll be safer, working in Europe this way."

In her next letter, Frieda wrote back: "I surely don't mind that you've changed your name. I want my boy to be a safe as possible. But I would appreciate it if my boy would only tell his mother what his new name is so I'll know to whom I should address future correspondence!"

Before leaving Fort Ritchie, Fred went to the courthouse in Hagerstown, Maryland to officially change his name. He felt a twinge of guilt as the clerk stamped his paperwork. Was he betraying his ancestry? What would his father think? It was too late to reconsider.

After one last three-day leave at home on the chicken farm, Fred reported to his ship in New York harbor. The troop carrier set sail in the afternoon, heading due east into the Atlantic, its destination unknown to the men on board. That night, Fred dreamt of his last ocean voyage just a few short years ago. So much had happened in the interim, so much had changed. He had been a mere boy. Now there was no turning back — he was a man on his way to war.

When he woke in the morning sunlight was streaming in through the bunkhouse portholes. Fred shaded his eyes to look out and he saw that they were accompanied by many troop carriers, all surrounded by Navy destroyers. It was a large convoy. On the third day out of New York, the convoy came under attack by German submarines.

All hell broke loose. I had never seen or felt anything like it. The explosions seemed to come from nowhere, deafening bursts that rocked our ship like a child's toy boat. I remember feeling sick to my stomach but too frightened to even care. Several of our ships were hit, and some were sunk in front of our eyes. We were hit, too, but not badly damaged. Suddenly the riots of Camp Shenango didn't seem so bad.

Days later, following even worse attacks, the troops cheered at the sight of the English coast. Fred was standing nearby when the first English officer boarded the troop carrier. He heard the man ask, "How many dead? How many injured?" in a matter-of-fact tone. Luckily, they had none. Many men were lost on other ships in the convoy.

Fred's unit was assigned to a replacement camp in Somerset County. From there, intelligence personnel were reassigned to different units. As always, it was a waiting game, only now, after the horrors they had witnessed at sea, the wait seemed more ominous. One morning Fred's orders arrived, directing him to London and a building on Grosvenor Street.

It was a very strange building with no signs, no identification at all on the outside, not even an American flag. On the train from Somerset to London, I had made friends with a soldier who was going on leave. The way he described it, I couldn't wait to go out for some fun on the town. I told him that I just had to report in and then I would probably have a few days to goof off.

"Just wait for me out here on the street in front of the building," I said. "I'll sign in and be right out."

Fred never came out of the front door of that building again. Upon entering, his identification was checked, and he was told to report to a naval officer in an office on the second floor. The officer, a man not much older than Fred, interviewed him. During the session, he asked, very abruptly, "You're Jewish, aren't you?"

Fred felt his ears begin to burn. It wasn't the question that bothered him, but the tone. He replied, "Yes, do you mind?"

The young officer just smiled and said, "No, my friend, we don't mind. Hitler may not like it, though."

Several more interviews followed. Fred lost all track of time. At least twice he asked if he could get a message to his friend not to wait any longer, but no one paid any attention. After the interviews, he was sent to a small laboratory where he was told to disrobe for a medical examination. Once they had determined that he was in perfect health, though rather short in stature compared to most American soldiers, he was allowed to don a fatigue uniform with no insignia whatsoever.

Along with several other recruits, I was taken to another location in the building. By this time, I had walked up and down so many corridors that I wasn't exactly sure where I was in relation to the front door I had entered.

We were ushered into a small auditorium without seats. On the low stage in front of us stood a man I immediately assumed was the commanding officer. There was no way to really tell because everyone at this place wore uniforms like ours, without insignia, completely nondescript.

"Welcome all of you," the officer said. "When you entered this place, you left your name, rank, serial number and your honor behind. We will teach you what your mothers never thought you should know — to steal, to crack safes, to pick pockets, even murder. No one here has a rank. We'll address each other by first names only." He paused to survey the faces of his new recruits. No surprises there, as always the boys looked dumbfounded, as if they doubted their own sanity. "Any questions?"

Chapter Ten

The training was tough. It left Fred mentally and
physically exhausted each night, but it also left him with an
incredible sense of satisfaction. It was a far cry from those
uncertain days at Camp Shenango. He learned to shoot every
weapon in both the Allied and enemy arsenals. He learned to
do things his mother would surely not have approved of; and
he learned them all quite well. In fact, Fred discovered he had a
special talent for such activities as "gutter fighting" and safe
cracking.

Fred passed each test and completed his training. He was
sent back to London and assigned to a billet in the Chelsea
District. The Germans had just begun air raids with their new
V1 rockets, which were soon to be followed by the V2. The V1
looked like a small airplane with a jet engine. Cruising toward
its target, suddenly the engine would stop. The rocket would
continue a short distance and then drop to the ground with a

tremendous explosion. One could see the V1 approaching, but once its engine stopped, it was impossible to know where it would drop. The later and more advanced V2 could not be seen.[5]

I vividly recall the first V1s dropped over London. It was early one morning before I had left for the office. We heard the sound and went up to the roof to see what was happening. It looked like a small plane on fire was coming toward us, slightly to the south. Then the flames stopped and it dropped out of sight, only to be followed by an enormous explosion about six blocks away. Soon another came, this time to the north of where we stood, watching in dumbfounded fascination. It too dropped out of sight and exploded.

"If this is like artillery fire, the next target would be right in the middle," said one of Fred's neighbors, an artillery expert,

---

[5] Guided missiles were an important German technical achievement during World War II. By 1941 German scientists were testing a missile called the *Vergeltungswaffe 1* (Vengeance 1, or V1) that used a jet engine and relied on a type of "autopilot" for guidance. It was about 29 feet in length and weighed almost 5,000 pounds. The V1 was first launched in the summer of 1944, and over the next several months, thousands were directed toward London. Allied pilots gradually learned ways to down some of the missiles.

The V2, a liquid-fueled rocket with a longer range and greater payload than the V1, traveled much like a modern rocket ship—flying nearly straight up, reaching the border of space and falling nearly straight down at speeds faster than sound. At the time, there was no way to stop such a missile or even detect its approach.

who lived two floors below.

"That's us!" Fred said. And the group rushed downstairs, practically falling over each other to get out of the building.

Nothing happened immediately, and since it was time for Fred to go to work anyway, he walked on to his office. By the time he arrived at his desk, word had been received that a bomb had made a direct hit on his building. He rushed back to what had once been home. It was a terrible sight. Fire engines and rescue squads were already on the scene, but everything was destroyed. Several people had been injured — two were dead. The only possessions Fred had left were the clothes he was wearing.

Soon after the V1 rocket wiped out my first London residence, I was given a generous clothing allowance of $210 and a per diem of $5.50 for food. My orders were to live on the civilian economy with no access to military installations. I was issued an identification card that said simply "Embassy of the United States, London. "

Fred was given a week off to get used to being a civilian again. When he reported back one week later, they told him to take another week off. He was beginning to think it was a great war. Later he learned that his security clearance had been delayed and, until it arrived, he was simply not welcome at headquarters. The same was true for several other young recruits, two of whom, Bill Selvig and Jerry Gutmann, became Fred's good friends. They had all volunteered for the U.S. Office of Strategic Services (OSS), and since they found themselves fancy free, they decided to have as good a time as possible.[6]

Almost every day, the three young men could be found at the Hotel Piccadilly tea dance. In the evening, they frequented a number of popular dinner clubs. Fred had found a new apartment conveniently located in Kensington, not far from Hyde Park.

For a short while, Bill, Jerry and I were like college students without classes to attend. It was common practice at the time for Allied military police to check the IDs of young people in civilian clothes. Once a woman we had seen around approached us and asked why we were not in the service. We told her we worked for the U.S. Embassy.

"What do you do there?" she asked.

Bill and Jerry hesitated, but Fred jumped right in, "We're the chief window washers."

A few days later, Fred received a call from his section chief at OSS headquarters. "Rodell," he said, gruffly, "try to come up with some better story for yourself. Window washers, indeed! My six-year-old son could have done better."

The woman, it turned out, was an OSS operative.

A few days later, still on extended leave, Bill and Fred

---

[6] The Office of Strategic Services was launched during World War II by General William J. Donovan under the Joint Chiefs of Staff, with the approval and support of President Franklin D. Roosevelt. Its goal was to improve, coordinate and provide intelligence needed for wartime activities. Branches of the OSS included SI (Secret Intelligence), SO (Special Operations), OG (Operational Groups) and MO (Morale Operations).

had dinner at one of their favorite clubs. After their meal, while they waited for the band to begin playing while scanning nearby tables for potential dates. It appeared to be their lucky night. Two very well-groomed young ladies were just finishing their own meals.

I told Bill that when the music started, he should ask the tall one to dance and I would ask the other one. We waited and watched, trying not to be too obvious about our interest. I saw "my girl" ask the waiter for the check. As soon as she had paid it, Bill and I moved in. The band had begun to play, and the two girls were getting up to leave.

"Ladies," Bill said, turning up his charm, "You can't leave so soon. The music is just starting."

"Yes," Fred chimed in, "The night is young."

Bill took the taller girl's hand and led her toward the dance floor. Fred's girl seemed annoyed at first, but soon they joined the other couples, swirling around the dance floor to the big band sounds. Fred's choice had been dictated almost entirely on the basis of height, something he was apt to do considering he stood only five feet tall. This time, however, the match worked out better than he could have expected.

Joyce and I seemed a perfect match. She was just slightly taller than I was. Her smile, when she finally decided to smile at me, made my knees go weak. I can still remember how soft she felt in my arms and how her perfume filled the air around us.

After several dances, the four young people took a table together. Fred ordered and paid for the first round of drinks — champagne cocktails for the ladies, whiskey and soda for the OSS recruits. It was a magic night; everything seemed to click, and they wound up closing the place.

I made a date with Joyce for the next evening. After that we were together almost every evening until my orders sent me away. Joyce was not only well educated; she was also wealthy. Of course that had nothing to do with my attraction to her. She had an art degree and was well known in that circle. We attended far more art exhibits than I cared for, but being around her, listening to her talk and hearing her laugh at my jokes, made it worthwhile.

Joyce worked at a leading art gallery on Bond Street, just a few blocks from Fred's office. He would pick her up for lunch periodically and always be waiting for her at six o'clock for dinner and dancing. One evening, while he waited in the front of the gallery, Joyce was busy near the back with a tall, elegant looking woman. Their business concluded, the two women walked toward the door. Seeing Fred, Joyce stopped to introduce him to Queen Wilhelmina of the Netherlands, one of her regular customers.

Before long, Fred and Joyce were living together in his little room in Kensington. Before moving in, Joyce explained to Fred that she had been divorced for more than a year and had a one-year-old son, who stayed with her parents on their country estate. Joyce didn't want the baby in London during the continuing bombing raids.

I grew more and more serious about Joyce as time went by. Eventually, I asked her to marry me. She refused because of her son. She said she had vowed not to remarry until he reached the age of 21.

Chapter Eleven

Fred lived like a man of leisure in London for two more weeks before his security clearance arrived at OSS headquarters. By that time, he had begun his courtship of Joyce and was well acquainted with the streets and neighborhoods, cafés and nightclubs of his new home away from home. Duty called, however, and Fred was assigned to the Morale Operations branch, known simply as MO.[7]

The purpose of MO was "to create and disseminate black propaganda." Fred became part of an effort to supply information and disinformation to the people of Germany. It took many forms, from bogus newspapers and forged letters to daily radio broadcasts, most directed toward German and Fascist Italian troops in an attempt to weaken their spirit. German citizens were strictly forbidden to listen to foreign

---

[7] MO employees worked with "black" propaganda—disinformation that is deniable by (and not traceable to) its source. This technique became an effective tool for influencing enemy opinions and perceptions.

radio broadcasts. To get caught listening to foreign broadcasts would mean jail and probably death.

So, MO operated a radio station that went on the air as if it were a German station. To verify its authenticity, the staff would broadcast information collected from mail sent to German POWs. A mother might write to her son, for example, that a certain building in Munich had burned down and was totally destroyed. By including this information in one of its broadcasts, MO led people to believe it was an authentic German station.

We reported on Nazi excesses in obtaining food rations, the kind of abuse of power the common German knew was true. Then we would give them our slant on the news. We were so authentic that a Naval OSS intelligence officer in the office next to ours monitored us for several weeks before reporting in a mutual meeting that "Soldaten Sender West," which was our call signal, was not a German station. We know, we told him. That's us.

Another MO function was writing seditious anti-Nazi leaflets, forged military announcements and subversive letters. Fred worked side by side with a staff of talented writers producing everything including certificates and passes assuring proper treatment to soldiers who surrendered. These were particularly effective, as many German and Italian soldiers showed the passes upon their surrender. The total of known desertions directly caused by MO subversion was estimated at 10,000. Even more weighty evidence of MO's effectiveness was the frequent and violent German reactions to MO "black" propaganda.

Distribution of written propaganda took many ingenious forms. Carefully screened prisoners-of-war were sent back, still in German uniforms, to the front lines. Fake German mailbags were filled with subversive letters stamped, postmarked and inscribed with real addresses taken from local directories. These bags were strategically dropped by the Air Force and often wound up being sent on as stray mail pouches by the regular German mail. The device was apparently never detected by German authorities.

A number of very talented people worked at MO, including Ira Ashley, producer of the popular NBC Radio Series Grand Central Station. During Fred's brief tenure in the London MO office, he worked with American writer and historian Arthur Schlesinger, leading German publisher Gunther Ulstein, British comedian Dick Oliver, who was married to Sara Churchill, and, of course, the great Marlene Dietrich, who eventually recorded an album entitled, "Songs I Sang for the OSS."[8]

---

[8] As an OSS volunteer, Dietrich entertained Allied troops throughout World War II, often within firing range of enemy units. She recorded popular songs such as "Lili Marlene," "Miss Otis Regrets" and "The Surrey with the Fringe on Top" in German. The OSS broadcasted the recordings to German troops as part of a psychological warfare operation designed to lower their morale and fighting effectiveness. OSS director William Donovan extended his gratitude for Dietrich's help: "I am personally deeply grateful to you for your generosity in making these recordings for us."

Soon after the Normandy invasion, Fred was called into Colonel David Bruce's office. He was the OSS commanding officer in London, a man Fred had little previous interaction with beyond saluting him when they passed occasionally in the hallway.

Naturally I thought I had done something wrong. Maybe I was feeling a little bit guilty about how easy my life was going. My days of fabricating black propaganda in the MO office were downright fun, and by then Joyce was living with me so my nights were even more enjoyable.

"Fred, I need you to change into a real uniform and get down to Barrington Air Field immediately," Colonel Bruce said. "There's a plane standing by to take you to Cherbourg." He paused as if to let this sink in, and then said, "We need you to interrogate the first captured German general."

The colonel explained that the EEI, Essential Elements of Information, would be sent from the Joint Chiefs of Staff at any moment. "They'll be delivered to you at the airport. I want you to study them on the plane and I'll expect a full report from you when you get back."

Fred stood at attention in front of Colonel Bruce's desk, his mind racing with the realization that his first real mission was beginning. A flight to Cherbourg! He had never even flown before. And most incredible of all, he would be interrogating the first captured German general. Colonel Bruce looked up and barked: "Those are your orders, soldier. Get going at once!"

Within two hours, I was sitting on a C-47 transport plane. Just before we took off, an Air Force officer arrived and handed me a sealed Manila envelope stamped Top Secret. As the airplane lifted off, I broke the seal and started to read the EEI. I couldn't believe what I saw. All the information they wanted was about the Russians: size of troops, morale, who commanded them, what equipment they had, what condition it was in, etc.

I figured someone had really screwed up. Here we were, barely in France and with our first captured German general, and they wanted me to question him about who I thought were our allies — the Russians.

"Someone really flipped," Fred murmured to himself as he tore up the EEI. He proceeded to make comprehensive notes of his own on what he thought the Allies needed to know to provide its field commanders with more information on the real enemy — the Germans who were at that very moment retreating around the Cherbourg area.

Fred conducted his first interrogation in the backroom of a Cherbourg brothel, where makeshift intelligence headquarters had been set up temporarily. At that time, fighting was raging still nearby, and the sound of gunfire and the impact tremors of not-so-distant artillery fire punctuated the questioning.

He was a swarthy, middle-aged German from Berlin. I felt a surge of contempt for him the minute I saw his spotless uniform. He answered every question politely and appeared

103

unconcerned about passing along vital information about the German troops he had commanded. As I jotted down notes, I felt a wave of joy pass over me, to think I was finally doing something to make a difference.

Less than 24 hours after leaving, Fred was back in London. He had not slept except for a catnap on the airplane, but he went straight to his office and spent half the night writing his report. At six o'clock in the morning, he put the report on Colonel Bruce's desk and went home to shower before work.

At ten minutes after nine, a private came to Fred's desk at Soldaten Sender West. "Colonel Bruce wants to see you at once," he said.

Fred tried to remain poker faced but he couldn't resist a slight smile. He was certain Colonel Bruce would commend him for realizing that someone had made a terrible mistake. As soon as Colonel Bruce saw him, he held up the report and said, "What the hell is this?"

"Sir, someone in Washington really goofed and sent us the wrong EEI. All the questions they sent were about the Russians! As soon as I realized the mistake, I made up my own EEI."

Colonel Bruce rose from his chair and walked around his desk to stand directly in front of Fred, who remained at attention. "So, you're telling me that the Joint Chiefs of Staff goofed, is that it, Rodell?" The colonel, a relatively tall man at 6'2", bent over to thrust his face into Fred's. "You corrected them! You're telling the Joint Chiefs of Staff what they should know, is that it, Rodell?"

The good colonel was very unhappy. Washington wanted specific information immediately and Fred had blown it. What he didn't know then was that the German general had just been transferred to France from the Russian front. Washington wanted information on the Russian allies because even then they didn't trust them.

It was a dismal moment in my life, but I took comfort in knowing I wasn't the only one to make a mistake during those days with OSS in London. At a meeting less than a week earlier, the officer in charge of leaflet distribution was reporting how many leaflets had been dropped in Germany, France and Poland.

"I'm happy to report that we dropped 10,000 copies of leaflet B in Poland, 10,000 copies of leaflet A in France and 10,000 copies of leaflet C in Germany," the young officer announced proudly.

There were examples of each leaflet on the conference room table. A moment passed before everyone at the table began laughing uncontrollably, except the poor reporting officer. He had dropped German leaflets into Poland, Polish leaflets into France and French leaflets into Germany. The whole operation was a complete waste.

Chapter Twelve

William J. "Wild Bill" Donovan, the fabled head of the OSS and father of the Central Intelligence Agency (CIA), was open to taking chances. "If we make mistakes," he would say, "we'll learn from them and move forward."

Mistakes did happen, sometimes out of simple error, sometimes because security was so tight. Each night, for example, all the discarded papers in the MO office were collected by two officers and taken to a central location for shredding and burning.

One day, Fred was summoned to Colonel Bruce's office. The colonel had not yet forgiven Fred for his goof with the German general. When Fred arrived at his doorway, the colonel just sat there shaking his head.

"Rodell, you've disappointed me again," he said. "Last night you left a top secret document on your desk."

"Sir, I'm sorry, but I don't think I ever did that."

"Really? Well, Captain Wilson seems to think

otherwise." He held up a sheet of paper. "His report says he had to shred a rather large document after you left the office last night."

I was perplexed, and I had no good answer for the colonel. It wasn't until several days later that I realized what had happened. On the day in question, I had to classify a document pertaining to an upcoming broadcast we were planning on food shortages in the Nazi occupied countries. My rubber "Top Secret" stamp never worked well on the first try, so I tried it first on a copy of the London Times sitting on my desk. Ironically, it worked perfectly well that time and, without thinking about it, I left the newspaper on my desk that evening.

Captain Wilson must have come along, found the Times and assumed it was truly a top secret document. The next time I saw Wilson, I couldn't resist telling him that anybody could buy the London Times anywhere in England! He looked at me without smiling and said, "Not with a top secret stamp on it."

Shortly before Allied Forces marched into Paris, Fred was sent to the city to find suitable billets for OSS personnel. One of his colleagues on the trip was John Ringling North, of the famous circus family; the other was Navy Commander Walter Armour, one of the heirs to the meat-packing fortune. As soon as they arrived in Paris, they took over the luxurious Ritz Hotel. One of the world's finest hotels, it seemed the perfect place for the OSS advance team. Unfortunately, after one night in their opulent accommodations, the three men were unceremoniously evicted by aides to General Eisenhower, who was planning to use the famous hotel for his own headquarters.

It didn't take long for the OSS scouts to find another elegant hotel on the Champs Elysees. North was particularly fond of this location because it was a short walk from the *Maison Internacionale*, at that time the world's best-known first-class house of ill repute. He insisted that Fred and Walter accompany him there on a brief fact-finding mission. When they entered the front door, the madam rushed forward to embrace and kiss North, who was obviously well known and liked at the establishment.

When the great Allied march into Paris finally occurred on August 25, 1944, it was an unforgettable sight. From the balcony of the new OSS headquarters at #69 Champs Elysees, Fred and his cohorts watched the parade of soldiers being cheered by grateful Parisians. The City of Lights had been liberated at last, but the war was far from over.

Most of the time, we worked hard and did what we were supposed to be doing. My days at MO writing radio broadcasts and leaflets were over. Now we were preparing for a much more direct form of enemy infiltration and confrontation.

Some of us did, of course, take time out to make frequent visits to Mimi Pension, the little nightclub in the basement of our hotel headquarters. On one of our visits, at about three o'clock one afternoon, the waitress, Bridgette, who knew me well, pointed out a man at the bar. In a whisper she said, "He's a high ranking SS officer, a general or a colonel, I'm not sure which. He's hiding out in Paris." Without a moment's hesitation, I went over and placed the man under arrest. It wasn't difficult to take him in. He had been drinking heavily for days and appeared almost relieved when I slipped the handcuffs on his wrists. Immediately, I brought the man upstairs and presented him to Colonel Bruce.

"Where did you find this man?" the colonel asked Fred.

"Downstairs in Mimi Pension, sir." Fred replied.

Colonel Bruce glared at Fred. "What the hell were you doing in the nightclub at three o'clock in the afternoon, Rodell?"

Fred just shrugged. It seemed he would never get a commendation from Colonel Bruce, no matter how hard he tried. As the smallest man in the unit, he was determined to prove himself. He wanted to do more than back office analysis and paperwork, but feared his size and, now unfortunately, his growing reputation with Colonel Bruce, would keep him away from the sexier OSS duties.

Within a week of the Mimi Pension arrest, one of the colonel's top aides informed Fred that he was to receive new orders in the colonel's office in the morning. "Don't dare be late, Fred, he'll hang you out to dry if you're not waiting outside his door at eight."

"Listen, Tom, you can be straight with me, what has the colonel got in store for me?" Fred asked.

The look that came across Tom's face should have tipped me off. The biggest adventure of my life was about to begin.

PART TWO

Behind Enemy Lines

Chapter One

André was already in the colonel's office when I arrived at 7:45 a.m. I hadn't met him, but I knew his reputation. "I want you to meet André Pacatte," Colonel Bruce said. "He's your new partner."

Fred was speechless for a moment, a rare state of affairs. He was recalling the many stories he'd heard about the legendary French spy André. He was a big man, at least 6'2", with close-cropped, sandy hair and piercing ice blue eyes.

"Aren't you supposed to be in the Mediterranean?" Fred finally blurted out, trying his best to appear calm.

"I've been transferred here now," André explained, his voice betraying only a slight French accent.

The colonel observed the two men, and Fred wondered what he was thinking. Was this assignment the colonel's way of getting him back?

"Before we go into any details of your assignment, why don't you two go out, have a cup of coffee and get better acquainted?" Colonel Bruce suggested. "We'll meet back here at 1030."

They went to Mimi Pension in the basement, and Fred considered ordering a glass of wine to calm his nerves. Before he could say anything, André told Bridgette to bring them two black coffees and two shots of anisette, a licorice-flavored liqueur. Fred started to say something and then let her go. He looked across the table at André. The man seemed to loom over him like a mountain.

"I heard about your adventures on the coast of Africa," Fred said.

"What did you hear?"

"They say you pulled off some pretty slick maneuvers."

André laughed. "Is that what they say?"

"Yes. Supposedly you commandeered an Italian submarine that had come over to our side. You forged an official-looking seal from a half dollar and a potato, and the Italian sub captain bought it."

André shrugged.

"The way the story goes, you approached the captain and told him you needed to use his sub. He said he was under Allied orders, and you handed him the counterfeit orders rather than go through the trouble of getting real ones."

"I wanted to get the job done before the war ended, so I did what I had to do."

Fred nodded.

"Look, Fred," André said, leaning across the small table,

113

"My philosophy is, let's worry about what is ahead of us, not behind. I did some crazy stuff during my last assignment. Things were different then. We didn't know what was going to happen or if the invasion of North Africa would succeed. Now look at us. We're in Paris, for God's sake! We've got the Nazis on the run. I want to get through this war alive if at all possible."

Again Fred nodded. He was beginning to like André.

André continued, "As my partner, I want you to swear to do what I tell you and don't do anything stupid."

The coffee and anisette came and André kept on talking. It was a big patriotic speech: We're going to win this war and we're going to do this and that, but we're going to do it with our heads firmly planted on our shoulders. "I want us both to live to play with our grandchildren," were the last words he said before downing his anisette and signaling to Bridgette for another. I assured André that I was in full agreement.

Back in Colonel Bruce's office at 10:30 a.m. sharp, André and Fred learned that their mission would be to work simultaneously for MO and Secret Intelligence (SI). Their principal activity would be the recruitment and training of agents from the pro-Allied French population to infiltrate behind German lines. The two agents would be sent to obtain strategic information on German military units, order of battle, troop and general population morale in German-occupied areas.

Colonel Bruce stopped briefly and sniffed at the air. "I smell licorice," he said. "Do you smell that?"

Both André and Fred shook their heads and after a moment, the colonel continued: "We need to know the Germans' positions and armaments; any military information that can be extracted. The civilians you'll be training have friendly contacts with high ranking German officers. It will be dangerous for them, but they represent our best opportunity. Any questions?"

"When do we start?" Fred asked.

"Immediately."

Our orders were to follow the Third Army, which was just outside Nancy, a few hours east of Paris. André was born and raised in the area, which explained his transfer. Although we were partners, he would be calling the shots, and he took charge by immediately arranging the necessary supplies and transportation for our mission. At the motor pool, we took delivery of a jeep, trailer and several five-gallon cans. At the supply depot we were given a foot locker full of French francs, handguns, a submachine gun, ammunition, hand grenades and, of course, a radio.

They left for Nancy immediately. It was normally a two-hour drive from Paris, but along war-gutted roads the going was much slower. Occasional artillery fire could be heard in the distance in the direction that Fred and André were heading. Fred commented at one point that it was like driving toward a fierce thunderstorm you could hear but not yet see. Not far from the city limits, they encountered an army patrol and were told that the city officially belonged to the Allies.

General Patton had issued orders not to drink the water in Nancy for fear that the retreating Germans may have poisoned the water supply. Soldiers were worried about encountering booby traps behind every door they opened.

André bypassed Army headquarters and drove directly to the address of the pro-de Gaulle group, one of three French intelligence services operating in the area. André and Fred were instructive to work exclusively with this group, not the anti-de Gaulle or Communist bands.

It was a somewhat uneasy introduction. The French operatives were understandably suspicious at first. For one thing, neither Fred nor André appeared to be Americans. Also, with the liberation of Nancy only hours old, everyone was especially suspicious — German spies were expected behind every door where there was no booby trap. But after the two identities were verified, French leaders pledged their full support. André explained their goals: to identify pro-Allied civilians who had close contact with German officers during the occupation and recruit and train them to operate behind enemy lines. Their French contact started preparing a list of prospects.

That night André and I moved into our assigned billet, which was on the third floor of a small, three-story apartment building near the main square. It was a nicely furnished two-bedroom apartment with living and dining room, kitchen and balcony. As we entered the dining room, we noticed that the table was set for four with knives, forks, spoons and plates, a fresh tablecloth, spotlessly clean. In the bedrooms, there were fresh linens on the beds. Obviously, the previous occupants — German officers and their girlfriends — had left rather hurriedly. Some German uniform garments as well as ladies' clothing still hung in the closets. The kitchen was well-stocked with specialty items unavailable elsewhere in France: chocolate, coffee and other delicacies. I couldn't help but remember the radio broadcasts about the plight of French civilians under German occupation — but food shortages had not affected the invading army.

While inspecting the pantry, Fred found cases of the finest French liqueurs: Benedictine, Armagnac, Cointreau and Napoleon cognac, each case clearly marked "for German military consumption only." Those bold red letters stamped on each case seemed like a direct challenge. Having been in the jeep all day, both André and Fred were extremely thirsty, but General Patton's standing orders forbade them from quenching their thirst with water from sources not already under allied control.

Tired as I was, and not being a connoisseur, I popped open a bottle of Benedictine, filled a water glass and said to André, "Let's drink this stuff." He looked at me like I was a fool. "You can't drink that. It will only make you thirstier, and soon you'll keel over." I chose to ignore his warning. What can I say? I was young and inexperienced. Within a very short time, after stubbornly downing an entire glass of what I refused then to admit was a foul-tasting liquid, I did keel over.

André watched Fred drink the Benedictine with an amused look. It had been awhile since he had seen such naiveté, yet he had to admit the kid had moxie. That would serve them both well in the weeks ahead. Around 9 p.m., Fred got violently ill and threw up in the Germans' spotless bathroom. By 10 p.m., André had deposited him between the sheets of a perfectly made bed in one of the immaculate bedrooms.

From the moment his head hit the soft, fragrant pillow, Fred was dead to the world. He recalled no dreams that night and did not awaken in the wee hours to pee, let alone in response to the thunder and lightning of artillery fire outside.

When I woke up the next morning, I looked up from my luxurious bed at the morning sky. The chandelier was lying on the foot of my bed amid a clutter of paint chips and roofing tiles. The apartment was wrecked. André came in and said, "You're damn lucky to be alive!"

"What the hell happened here?" Fred shouted, immediately regretting the noise of his own voice.

"At midnight we were bombarded by the German railway guns for about 45 minutes. I tried to get you out of bed. Some of our neighbors even came in to help, but you told us to leave you alone, you weren't going anywhere. We decided to seek shelter because we knew another round was coming. And it did. This building got a direct hit. The attic above us is completely destroyed. I didn't think I'd even find your body when we came back." André stared at Fred like in wonderment. "You're damn lucky, and I'll tell you one thing. I want your luck to rub off on me."

After Fred swallowed a handful of aspirin with fresh water that André had acquired from the neighbors, the two men set to work trying to return their apartment to some semblance of order. A short while later, two middle-aged women appeared at their open door, saying they were maids and offering to cook and clean for a reasonable price.

"We are so happy the Americans have come to liberate us," said one of the women. "We were forced to work for the German soldiers who lived here before you. They never paid us."

Already bored with housework, André and Fred hired them on the spot, and in no time the place looked as good as new. Workmen arrived to repair the roof and attic, and one of the new maids prepared a hearty breakfast of potatoes and eggs. Fred had not known such domestic bliss since he lived at home with his mother and uncle in Vineland.

Chapter Two

Fred and André began their mission by telling their first lies. Hoping to speed up the process and accomplish their goals more efficiently, they decided to pay visits to the other French intelligence service, known as the *Deuxiéme Bureau*.[9] Fred went to one and André went to the other. At both, the leaders insisted on being given assurances that the Americans would only work with them and not the other two. Without blinking an eye, André and Fred told them both what they wanted to hear.

> *We gave them all the same assurances because we were not interested in their politics; we didn't care if they were for de Gaulle, against de Gaulle or Communist. As long as they were against the Germans, we figured they were on our side. We needed agents that could be trusted.*

---

[9] The *Deuxiéme Bureau de l'Etat-major général* (Second Bureau of the General Staff) was France's external military intelligence agency from 1871 to 1940. It was dissolved upon the armistice with Germany.

Late that afternoon, André and Fred met at U.S. military headquarters to obtain special passes. Nancy was under a strict curfew, and no one was permitted in the streets after dark without proper authority. The passes would allow them to contact prospective agents secretly at their homes at night.

Within a day I made my first contact. It also happened to be the first time I became acquainted with gunfire. About 11 o'clock, I followed the directions I had been given to the home of my contact. I was very anxious to be on time. The streets were pitch black with no moon out and, of course, the city was completely blacked out. I had lain out the route with great care. As I walked through the streets, suddenly I heard a single shot fired behind me. I spun around and saw the burst of gunfire as several more shots directed at me erupted from a darkened doorway. Instinctively, I pulled my own pistol from my belt, returned a couple of shots and then ran like hell.

Fred's guardian angel was clearly on his shoulder that night. Later, he would learn that although Nancy was "liberated," a group of French pro-Germans remained. Apparently, they had already targeted him.

He arrived at his rendezvous safe and sound, though somewhat nervous, knowing he would have to return home via the same route after his meeting. By running most of the way, he had managed to arrive early. He knocked on the door, keeping one eye over his shoulder. The man who answered was

Claude, a member of the pro-de Gaulle group, who had arranged for Fred to meet Colette, his first prospect.

She turned out to be a lady of the evening. The house where we met was known as a "house of horizontal refreshment." The room, which smelled of perfume, had been recently redecorated with French, British and American flags.

Colette was an attractive young woman with short, curly black hair and dark, seductive eyes. She spoke German well and wasted no time telling Fred her story.

"I was born in a very small town near the German border," she began. "My mother was killed by the Germans when the war began. My father was deported by the Germans. I don't know where they took him. I hope he is still alive, but..." Colette gave a futile shrug as if to say she knew the chances were slim.

It was immediately obvious to Fred that Colette was well-educated. She spoke a few words of English, saying she had learned them as a schoolgirl before the war. After, alone and without financial support, she had become a prostitute to stay alive.

Colette had been "befriended" by a German colonel with whom she more or less lived for many months prior to the liberation. She had fed the Free French information periodically, anything she could dig up through her relationship with the colonel and his officers. She pulled a tattered scrapbook from under the bed to show Fred evidence of her German contacts — photographs taken with the colonel and recent letters. Pointing to the colonel in one of the pictures she called him *mein schönes deutsches Schwein* — my nice German pig.

I let her talk all she wanted, taking a few notes. When she stopped, I asked, "How do you think you can help our cause?"

"I'll do anything you want me to do!" Colette insisted in a loud voice.

Fred nodded, reached out to pat her hand and smiled. Her emotional response worried him. He needed his agents to remain levelheaded at all times. "I'm sure we'll find some way for you to help us," was all he said.

"Where are you staying?" Colette asked, as Fred prepared to leave.

"Not far from here."

"Be careful going back," she warned. "Parts of this neighborhood can be dangerous."

"Really? Which parts?"

Colette went to the window and pulled the curtains slightly back. "Several blocks to the south of here there are German collaborators." She sneered.

"How do you know this?" Fred asked, remembering the gunfire.

"I saw these men with the Germans. They gave *mein Schwein* information about the activities of the resistance. I contacted the Free French to let them know about these cowardly traitors."

"Who did you contact in the resistance?"

Colette gave Fred several names without hesitating. It was becoming increasingly clear that she was going to be an excellent resource. She was extremely observant and her good looks would surely make her welcome when she crossed back over the front line to rejoin her German colonel.

Fred left Colette's and returned home through the dark streets, all the way expecting to hear more gunfire. He saw no one and heard nothing, much to his relief. At home André was hanging up his jacket, having also just returned from a hard evening of recruiting.

"It's not the job I mind so much," André said, yawning. "It's the hours."

Fred spent the next few days investigating Colette. He began by talking with each of the resistance members whose names she had given him. He was determined to be absolutely certain, not wanting to take any chances that she might turn into a double agent. As each reference checked out, he resolutely moved on to the next.

While Fred continued his meticulous investigation of Colette, André quickly recruited several agents. Three days later André confronted Fred, "What's wrong with you, Fred? I've already got five agents ready for training and you're still checking out one prostitute."

"I know I know," Fred answered, shaking his head. "I've completed her security check and I think she's going to be just fine, but I don't understand how you check your prospects out so quickly. I don't believe you're doing it by the book."

André smiled. "It's true," he said. "I don't need the

book. I have a secret weapon."

"What's that?"

André hesitated.

"Come on, man, you can't hold out on me, I'm your partner!"

"For one thing, I have more experience at this game than you do. You're a greenhorn."

"There's more going on here than that and you know it."

"Yes. You see, Fred, my job is done for the most part before I even meet the candidate."

"That's a neat trick. Now get on with it and tell me how you do it."

"I will tell you," he responded. "You will notice that none of my people are from Nancy, but from another town not too far from here, a town called Luneville. You didn't know this, but I was born in Luneville, and so were my father and mother and their parents. I grew up in this town until I immigrated to the United States. Most of my male family members were Freemasons. When I was old enough, I became a Freemason too. Many of my relatives are still in Luneville. All of my leads come through them and through the Freemasons. Every one of them has been involved in the in the underground either directly or indirectly. As you know, the Freemasons were persecuted by the Nazis and the French fascists just like the masons in Germany."

Knowing André's secret didn't help me very much at all. I couldn't help wondering, though, if someday I might be in the same position, recruiting agents from my hometown of

125

Nuremberg. It seemed unlikely. Most of my relatives had left Germany or wound up in concentration camps because they were Jews. I thought about friends of mine who were not Jewish. They would most likely be in the German army now. And I seriously doubted that I could trust the former friends of my family, since they either voluntarily or involuntarily became good Nazis. At that point I had no idea of the role my hometown would play in the war and its aftermath, or of the role I would play. I set my mind to the task at hand, determined to hold my own as a spy recruiter.

In the following days, Nancy received nightly bombardments by the German railway guns. Conditions worsened. The Third Army advanced to the outskirts of Metz. Information from underground sources indicated that the Germans were preparing to retreat from that city and move further north.

Patton's army had been advancing quickly, too quickly. It literally ran out of gas. For André and Fred this situation was both good and bad – good in the sense that they now had more time to develop their network of spies but bad because they too were very much restricted in the amount of gasoline they were given by the army. In fact, the amount rationed to them would not get them very far from their apartment.

"All I can give you is five gallons," the supply officer told them that first day.

"What the hell do you expect us to do with five gallons of gas?" André bellowed.

The soldier only shrugged.

Fred tried to use logic without revealing any details of their mission. "You can see that we have a trailer filled with five gallon containers and our orders say we're supposed to get anything we need. We've got an important mission to accomplish."

The supply officer was unimpressed.

"Don't you people realize there's a war going on?" Fred shouted, forgetting about logic. "I want to see your commanding officer right now!"

"You can see Old Blood and Guts himself, and he'll probably throw you both out of his headquarters on your asses," was all the supply officer would say.

Knowing Patton's reputation, we suspected the man was right, so we gracefully retreated to our apartment. To console ourselves, we supplied the maids with enough cigarettes and chocolates we had obtained from the PX for them to fill our pantry from the black market. We had no idea where they found the food, but they were able to offer us an incredible menu, and they were great cooks. They told us the Germans had taken their butter to grease their vehicles while the French were forced to eat dry bread. We made a practice of providing our maids and our recruits with adequate food for themselves and their families.

Fred and André continued to meet with the candidates on foot, always in different locations, never in the apartment. Each day they visited the supply depot to fill another five-gallon can with their daily ration until they had saved enough to make a trip to Luneville.

It was a cloudy afternoon. Fred buttoned his coat up to his neck to keep warm in the Jeep as André drove them along rutted roads. Along the way, Fred gazed at the passing scenery, feeling like a sightseer on a pleasant country drive. His mind wandered back to similar trips across Italian back roads he traveled as a young student. How far away in time and space all that seemed now.

Once we reached Luneville, our first order of business per André was to have a meal with his family — mother and father, a younger sister and two male cousins who had lost their parents to the war. They were all hearty country people with excellent taste in food and a healthy attitude about how to deal with the Nazis. I was amazed by the way our conversation shifted from old family recipes for asparagus and cream sauce to how best to sabotage German troops. It was overall quite a satisfying meal.

By five o'clock, André and Fred were at the small garage of André's first candidate, a mechanic in his early 40s. Pierre had done some favors for German officers during the occupation, keeping their stolen French cars in good working order. Shortly before the liberation, he was arrested for placing a bomb under a German officer's staff car. He was scheduled to be shot, but advancing American troops put a snag in the Nazis' plans for Pierre.

Standing in Pierre's tiny garage on the edge of town as the evening began to settle over Luneville, Fred listened to his tale. "I'm anxious to help you any way I can," Pierre said in conclusion. "I have a guardian angel who saved me once, and I believe he'll keep me safe. I can be a real asset to you. The officers I knew in Luneville still trust me, I'm certain of it. They know nothing of my little escapade."

On our way to meet some other candidates, I told André I thought this guy would work out well for us provided the Germans never discovered what he had done in the other town. "You're right," he agreed. "But if they do find out, they'll make him talk or cut his balls off."

Before the day ended, they had talked with two more candidates, both female and both of the same profession as Colette. They also seemed to have the right contacts among German officers. Most important, they genuinely despised these men.

During the interviews, André and Fred made absolutely sure that none of the candidates knew about the others. For security reasons, they could never get to know each other. Their individual training over the next few weeks included a lengthier question and answer period to learn everything about them and their connections with the German officers so that an infiltration strategy could be developed. Each agent needed an ironclad cover story, but the specific mission would remain a secret even to that individual until shortly before they went behind the lines to carry it out.

After my first visit to Luneville, I had a new respect for

André. He truly had recruited several people in so short a time and they all checked out. Both of the women, for example, were widows whose husbands had worked for the Free French and had been killed. They did not know each other, but they knew what their husbands had fought and died for, and they wanted to carry on the battle.

Chapter Three

André and Fred continued to search for recruits and train those who had cleared their security screening. Meanwhile the war progressed. Patton got the gasoline he needed, but not before the Germans found out about his predicament, reinforced their troops in Metz and counterattacked. It was a terrible fight, but once the Third Army had fuel, the tables turned again in the Allies' favor.

In Nancy the change in fortunes meant relief from the nightly bombardments and gasoline for the Jeep again became plentiful. Word arrived that a group of OSS agents was on its way to Luxembourg to establish a safe house. Over dinner in their apartment one evening, André and Fred discussed the news. To get to Luxembourg from Nancy would mean crossing a zone where battles were still raging.

"You up for it?" André asked, with a spoonful of soup poised before his mouth.

Fred finished chewing on a piece of buttered bread before he answered: "Absolutely. We leave in the morning."

We drove north in our Jeep pulling the well-stocked trailer behind us. Near Yutz, a section of the road had gone back and forth between Allied and Nazi control. They had warned us about it at Army headquarters and told us to check with the division intelligence officer to make sure it was safe to pass. Just before noon, we stopped at the small cluster of tents that made up field headquarters.

At the division intelligence officer's tent, they were met by a young corporal who told them the road had been clear that morning. "Just drive quickly," he said. "You'll be within small arms range."

Walking back to the jeep, André asked, "What do you think, Fred?"

"We've got to get there, don't we? Let me drive and you'll see how fast we can go."

So they headed on their way at top speed. Fred drove as fast as he could on the badly rutted road. André navigated with a map on his lap. Along the way they encountered deep bombed-out craters that were impossible to cross. Fred didn't hesitate. He swung the vehicle onto cross-country detours that eventually led back to the dirt highway.

On one curve, they suddenly heard a loud bang. The jeep went into a skid and, in what seemed like no time, turned over. They found themselves upside down in a ditch by the side of the road. André crawled out first and propped his back against a tree; he was bleeding from the head. Fred tried to follow him but couldn't; he was pinned under the jeep, unable to move his legs.

I remember seeing the blood trickling down André's face and thinking I needed to bandage his head immediately. I called out to him, "I have a bandage for your head… but I can't seem to move!" He crawled over and with his bare hands pulled my legs out from under the jeep. By some miracle, neither one of us was seriously hurt. The cut on his head was not much more than a scratch, and I bandaged it quickly.

"Look," André said, pointing west and then holding his finger up to his lips for silence. A German platoon with bayonets fixed was moving cautiously down the road toward the overturned vehicle.

I saw André reach for his gun, but it wasn't in his holster. When the Jeep turned over, the weapon had tumbled away. Between the two of us we had only one gun. In the vehicle we had all kinds of paperwork, including the names and addresses of our recruits and their German officer contacts.

"If they see us, fire into the gas tank. We have to blow up the jeep," André said, as calmly as he might have asked me to pass the soup at our dinner table. I knew he was right. We were in no condition to put up a fight and would have no choice but to surrender.

The German soldiers moved slowly and cautiously closer. Fred completely forgot the pain in his legs as he imagined what life as a prisoner of war would be like. Suddenly, a platoon of U.S. Army infantry appeared, storming over a small hill beyond the road. Several of the German soldiers were killed; the rest retreated, disappearing into the woods.

An American infantry sergeant stepped around the overturned jeep and leveled his weapon at Fred and André. "Stand up and put your hands on your heads," he said.

He thought we were Germans wearing American uniforms. Neither André nor I said a word. His accent was French, mine was German; speaking would only have aggravated the situation. He marched us to where some other GIs were holding prisoners, real prisoners. A truck came along and we were put on the back and brought to the rear where prisoners were interrogated. While we were waiting, neither the Germans nor the Americans would talk to us. The Germans could tell we were not from their side and the Americans thought we were their enemies.

Fred began to feel impatient. He finally turned to the guard and asked if he could smoke. The guard nodded, yes. When Fred pulled his pack of cigarettes from his breast pocket, the guard became belligerent.

"Chesterfields, eh?" He shoved Fred hard with the butt of his rifle. "You probably took them off one of the Americans you bastards killed!"

Fred left the fallen pack of cigarettes on the ground and

kept silent.

During their interrogation, Fred and André tried to explain who they were and what they had been doing. Unfortunately, their orders were in the overturned jeep. They related how they had inquired at Army headquarters and again at Division, but they didn't have the name of the corporal with whom they had spoken. The interrogating officer looked dubious, but he sent someone to look for the corporal.

Two hours later the corporal arrived. The interrogators brought Fred and André back out to the interrogating officer's tent. "Do you know these men?" he asked the corporal.

The corporal peered at them for a second and said, "I don't really know them. They came to our tent at field headquarters asking questions about the condition of the road. I never saw either of them before that."

He was no help to us. We had no choice but to finally give the interrogating officer the name of Colonel Harries at Third Army Intelligence, who knew of our mission and could verify who we were. Somehow they contacted him and asked him to come down to identify us.

More hours passed. The unhappy, misidentified prisoners just sat and waited as the sun went down. Fred finally picked up his crumpled pack of Chesterfields and began chain smoking them down to his fingers just for something to do. André didn't smoke. By the time Harries arrived, the pack was empty. The colonel shook his head in disgust when he saw the two OSS men, but without hesitating identified them as

American agents. They were released.

I followed André directly to the officers' mess. We hadn't eaten all day and we were famished. The food was only marginally edible, unidentified cubes of meat smothered in thick brown gravy and served with a pasty combination of beans and rice. We devoured it as if it was our usual gourmet fare.

It was so late they spent the night at the camp where they had been prisoners. Early the next morning, they were accompanied by several soldiers back to their Jeep to get their stuff. Fortunately, nothing was missing. André even found his gun wedged between the seats. The vehicle was useless and had to be towed into camp. That meant filling out extensive paperwork to get another vehicle, but by noon they were back on the road, heading north.

After the skirmishes of the previous day, the road was now firmly in Allied hands. Their adventure, it turned out, had taken place in Thionville, only 32 kilometers south of the border with Luxembourg. Even with the rough condition of the road, they arrived before sundown.

Luxembourg had only recently been liberated, and pandemonium still reigned in the streets. People welcomed the Americans and tried to give them bottles of wine. A well-dressed man stopped them and invited them to be his guest for dinner that night. He handed both André and Fred a copy of his card, ornately embossed with a coat of arms.

By four o'clock, they had met up with several other OSS

agents, who were operating a safe house, a large villa with a lovely garden located in a pleasant residential neighborhood.

As evening set, André and Fred walked back through the streets to the home of the man who had invited them for dinner. Along the way a parade of trucks with Luxembourg license plates passed noisily up and down the boulevards, carrying women with shaved heads. Hastily scribbled signs hung from the sides of the trucks identifying the women as "German Whores."

Dinner at the man's house turned out to be somewhat peculiar. The place was a mansion. André and I felt out of place in our wrinkled fatigues in the formal dining room with its crystal chandelier and hardwood sideboard. Nonetheless, I couldn't help but stare at a photograph of a young German soldier.

"I see you've taken note of my son's portrait," the host said to Fred.

"Your son?" Fred asked.

"Yes, my only son, Karl. He was forced to join the German army. It wasn't his choice or mine. He died on the Russian front."

After getting organized at the safe house, André and I returned to Nancy and made arrangements for our recruits to meet us at the Luxembourg address, two at a time. They were to travel there by their own means. At the assigned times, we drove back to Luxembourg to give them their orders and send them off into the field, behind enemy lines.

On the day Colette was scheduled to arrive, Fred worried that she would change her mind. But she arrived on time, complaining about what a difficult trip it had been. As instructed, she carried very few belongings.

André's recruit, Mimi, arrived from Luneville not long after Colette. They did not know each other. She spoke French and a little German. Unlike the petite Colette, she was a big-boned country girl, with thick waves of dark hair that fell across her face when she laughed.

According to procedure, André and Fred carefully checked out all of their belongings. What they found made it quite obvious that both girls had been kept by German officers – ample supplies of perfume, cosmetics and silk stockings, items that the ordinary French citizen could not have obtained at the time.

André took Mimi into one room; Fred took Colette into another.

"Colette," Fred began, "We have known each other only a short time, but I have all the trust and confidence in the world in you. I hope you feel the same way about me."

He was pacing slowly back and forth in front of her, watching her face for any reaction she might have.

"What I am asking you to do is no picnic. It may be very dangerous for you. I'm going to brief you as best I can. I hope you will be successful and return safely. You are about to become a soldier in the Allied force with the objective of defeating the Germans. If you have any doubts, now is the time to tell me."

"I have no doubts," Colette replied. "I want to do whatever I can."

"There's just one more thing I need to know from you," Fred said, stopping to look directly into her eyes. "If you have any financial obligations of any kind to anyone, a child perhaps, a relative or a business manager, you must let me know. Feel free. We will take care of whatever it is because we..."

Colette reacted at last, jumping up from where she sat on the edge of a bed. "You Americans think you can buy everything!" she shouted. "There is not enough money in the United States to buy my life. I am fully aware of what I am about to do and what I am doing I am doing strictly for France, no one else. I hope this is abundantly clear to you. I may be a whore, and I may have done things for money, but this is for France."

Fred smiled at her. "I never doubted you were a true patriot, willing to give your life for your country as I am. I only made you this offer because I want you to go about your duty with a clear head, no worries. I hope we can remain friends and comrades-in-arms."

Colette came to me then, embraced me and kissed me. It was more than a friendly kiss. We stepped away from each other, both embarrassed. Just then we heard a sound coming from the room next door.

Colette recognized the squeaking of bedsprings first and

she smiled at Fred. "*Votre ami travaille pour la France.*" Your friend is working for France.

They embraced and kissed again. As the night wore on, Colette and Fred also did their work for France.

I wasn't really expecting it, or even planning it, though it had surely been a long time since my last sexual encounter. Colette said she wanted to clean up a bit and went into the bathroom. When she came out, she was wearing a sexy negligee. We started to kiss again and then stumbled together onto the bed. For a long while, we let our bodies do the talking. Later, with her head nestled on my chest, I ran my fingers through her soft, black hair.

"Tell me now about my mission, Fred."

Fred sighed. "Yes," he said. "It's time."

He told Colette she was to cross the line on the pretext of getting away from the Americans and back with her German colonel. Once she found him, she was to stay with him as long as she could. When he said this, he felt Colette stiffen for a brief moment. She would, of course, be sleeping with him again, making him think that nothing had changed. The thought made Fred feel sick.

"You must find out anything and everything you can about the German troops," he continued. "We need exact numbers and of men, gun emplacements and fortifications. We need any data you can gather on troop morale. Are there weak spots, pockets of dissent? Are they expecting reinforcements? What other units, particularly SS units are in the area?"

Colette simply nodded her head as if nothing could be easier for her. As Fred went on, she rolled off him and lay next to him on her back, staring at the ceiling, while he told her to try to obtain documentation.

"Look for copies of battle orders," he said, "troop assignments and maps. As the fighting continues and we get closer, the asshole will have to retreat. When he does, hide the documents you've gathered, bury them, and avoid going with him. Stay put if you can and wait for our troops. You'll be able to contact me or André through any division intelligence officer. Or you can get someone to bring you back here, to this house."

In the dark, Fred turned to look at her, reached out and took her face in his hands. "If your colonel is reassigned or retreats, you must not go with him. It will be too dangerous and pointless. If you must, tell him at the last moment that you forgot something in the house, then run out the back way. He won't have time to look for you. You must find a way to come back toward the American line as quickly and cautiously as possible."

They dozed off in each other's arms. As the early morning light appeared in the cracks of the shuttered windows, Colette kissed Fred and they made love again. Afterwards, Fred whispered to her, "When you meet your colonel again, you must tell him how much you've missed him."

Colette laughed bitterly, "Don't worry. I know how to handle myself with him," she said.

Chapter Four

Fred drove Colette in the jeep as far north as he could go without crossing German lines. It was a dreary day, overcast and chilly with and occasional light drizzle that made everything feel wet. The war-scarred landscape they passed through was ominously quiet.

To tell the truth, I was scared shitless, but with Colette beside me I acted cool and calm. When we said good-bye, stopped along the side of the road with nothing but trees and pockmarked road stretching off ahead, I felt a sudden sense of guilt to be letting this young, fragile woman go forward into so dangerous and uncertain a situation.

Colette began walking northbound, picking her way around the muddy craters in the road, brown mud already clinging to her black shoes.

"Don't forget to wave your white handkerchief," Fred called after her.

"Of course I won't," she called back without turning.

"And the note," Fred called, standing up in the jeep. "Show them the note as soon as they stop you." She was carrying a note her German colonel had left her. In her small bag she also carried photographs of him and other personal items that would serve as ample evidence of her connection with the German officer.

"Goodbye, Fred." Colette called, stopping to turn around for the last time. From that distance, he could not tell if the streaks on her face were the result of tears or rain. Soon Colette was out of sight. Fred waited a while, listening for a reaction from the Germans he knew were just beyond the next rise in the road. When no sound came but the mournful call of some forest bird, he turned the jeep around and headed back to Luxembourg.

André and Fred returned to Nancy and continued recruitment and training. One by one their brave recruits set out on missions. Some returned soon with information; others never returned. Word came from one recruit that Colette had been seen out to dinner with her colonel in the town of Aachen. When he heard this, Fred felt joy knowing she had survived mixed with a strange twinge of jealousy that made him flush.

Just a few days before they were scheduled to leave Nancy, Fred and André began noticing people watching their apartment from the street below, men walking back and forth staring up at the windows. When André walked downstairs and went out to confront them, they quickly vanished down alleyways. As soon as he was back upstairs, they reappeared.

After 9 p.m. one evening, Fred went to get the jeep and trailer, which they had secretly loaded up with five-gallon cans of gasoline. A man he'd never seen before was standing by the garage door smoking a cigarette. When he saw Fred, he said, "I see you're getting ready to take a long trip."

"Why do you say that?" Fred asked him.

The trailer was tightly covered and locked, but the man seemed oblivious to this fact: "You've got plenty of gasoline on your trailer," he said, without offering any explanation.

Fred hurried back to the apartment and found André waiting at the front door with an anxious expression on his wide face. "We've got to get our asses out of here," he said.

"What's up?"

"Just take my word for it and pack quickly. We should leave now."

I assumed the pro-Germans were onto our operation and without asking any more questions, I tossed my already packed bag into the trailer and we drove through the dead of night out of Nancy. It wasn't until years later, when as a special investigator for the Nuremberg prosecution team I met one of the French freedom fighters in Strasbourg, and I learned the truth. The man recognized me and said, "You were in Nancy just after the occupation."

"That's right," I replied.

The man nodded and said, "We tried to get you for lying to us and collaborating with the anti-de Gaulle

*intelligence unit. We would have killed you and your big
friend if you hadn't disappeared so quickly."*

*Luckily, the war was over by then and all was
forgiven if not forgotten. We talked about old times and had
lunch together. The man turned out to be most helpful to
my investigations.*

André and Fred returned to Luxembourg and sent a
steady stream of recruits across the German lines. Almost all of
the recruits were ladies of the evening, except for one young
man. This fellow was an enigma to them; they couldn't figure
out how he had stayed out of the army. Since he was André's
recruit, Fred let it go during the training phase, but the night
before the boy was scheduled to cross over, he questioned
André.

André waved off Fred's questions. "He's a farm boy who
somehow slipped through official fingers and became a runner
for the resistance," André said.

Fred shook his head. "I don't like it one bit," he said.
"That story doesn't make sense to me."

André leaned forward and spoke in a harsh whisper.
"Listen, Fred, I couldn't care less what you think about him. I
have confidence in my sources on this boy. He's supposed to be
totally fearless and trustworthy. Those are features we need. So,
if he works out, fine. If not, too bad."

The day finally came when all the recruits were gone and
André and Fred had nothing more to do but return to
headquarters in Paris and report to Colonel Bruce. The story of
their sudden departure from Nancy was already well known by

the Colonel, but he seemed unconcerned about it and more pleased by their success at getting recruits into the field.

"An assault on Aachen is imminent," he said. "Now it's your turn to cross. Get your cover stories in order. I expect you to be in Aachen at least 24 hours before Patton."

Fred's cover was to be an Italian foreign worker and André a French worker. All of their documentation was ready.

During the entire trip north, André and I rehearsed our roles. At a prearranged spot, we stopped the jeep to get out of our uniforms and into civilian clothes. The local intelligence officer had been informed of our coming and a forward platoon escorted us as far as they could on foot. I remembered watching Colette head into danger. Now, I was the one walking into the unknown and my legs felt leaden, as if they would refuse to carry me.

The platoon left them at a convenient hiding place in a grove of trees at the base of a rocky hill. Then the handful of G.I.s moved east to where they would be within sight of the Germans. Less than three minutes passed before the Germans attacked and the platoon retreated, pursued by the Germans and leaving a very nice hole for André and Fred to pass through. In no time, they were behind the German lines.

It seemed too easy, and it was. The front line of Germans was made up of old men, known as the *Volkssturm*. Behind them was the regular army and behind them the SS troops. It was no big deal to get behind the *Volkssturm*. The real challenge would come later.

146

We started walking down a country road in the direction of Aachen. It was late afternoon and the sun was beginning to set. Up ahead, two German soldiers appeared out of nowhere. The moment they saw us they threw up their hands and shouted, "Halt!" We stopped in our tracks. As they approached us, one of them ordered me to step about 15 or 20 feet forward and to the left; they were separating André and me. They demanded to see our papers and questioned us. Of course my German was perfect, and the soldier seemed to believe my story. I couldn't help but notice that André, who spoke very little German, was having a harder time. I could tell from the sound of their voices that things were not going well, so I tried to keep my soldier occupied with small talk.

"My friend and I are headed to Aachen to make some money," I said, grinning. Out of the corner of my eye, I saw André make his move and my heart sank. There would be no turning back now. He grabbed the German, covering his mouth and turning him around in one swift motion. Like a flash, he slit the man's throat with his stiletto.

To this day I can see the blood spurting forth in a thick stream as if someone had turned on a faucet. The sound of his companion's body hitting the ground startled the soldier who had been calmly talking to me. He turned around and had just enough time to take in what had happened before I slipped my knife deep into his side with all the strength at my command.

It's true that in such circumstances you suddenly feel more strength than ever before. The sound he made as he died will never leave me. The entire affair was over in a split second.

"Come on," Fred shouted, "Let's get out of here."

Miraculously, they saw no other Germans as they fled the scene. Before they had gone very far, André grabbed Fred's arm to stop him. "Wait, wait, Freddie," he said, his voice so calm it shocked Fred, who felt a mixture of terror and revulsion.

"Wait? Are you crazy? Wait for what?"

"Maybe we should go back and get their papers to send to London."

"Forget it," Fred said. "I'm not going back there. There must be Nazis all over this place."

André peered at Fred with a curious grin. "You're so pale. Are you O.K.?"

"I've never killed a man before. Of course I'm not O.K."

André laughed. "If this war doesn't end soon, you'll get accustomed to it," he said. "It will get easy for you."

I didn't think so and I told André as much. But he continued to chuckle and treated me like a little boy as we hurried off toward Aachen.

Chapter Five

By the time they reached Aachen it was very late. Air raid sirens had just begun to sound in the small city. The two spies hurried through the unfamiliar streets to the first shelter they could find, in an apartment house. Close to the train station, it was a natural target, but they had to get off the street quickly to keep from arousing the suspicion of the air raid wardens, whose job it was to patrol the streets and make sure all citizens took shelter.

The people we followed into this shelter were all residents of the building, mostly women, with some old men and some young children. They soon asked us why we had come into their building, and I spoke for us both, giving them our foreign worker story. "We just got into town," I explained, shrugging. "Tomorrow we'll look for a place to stay, but for now, any port will do, no?"

At that moment, the first bombs began to drop quite close by, rocking the building above and causing the children to start screaming. André and Fred caught each other's eye, secretly cursing themselves for being so hasty and foolish in their choice of shelter. The building's residents were all well prepared with pillows and blankets. The two men had nothing and passed the night very uncomfortably.

As it turned out, we became trapped in this shelter for several days, as the Allied invasion roared above us on the streets of Aachen. When we tried to leave the next morning, our necks stiff from sleeping sitting up against the stone walls of the cold basement, we found ourselves in the middle of the battle. Allied troops were moving in, and the retreating German troops were making their last stand. André, who had emerged into the daylight first, quickly turned and pushed me back to the stairs. I heard bullets zing past the doorway where he had just been standing.

The residents welcomed them back. Having successfully crossed German lines, the two spies spent several days doing nothing more than making the close acquaintance of some humble civilian apartment dwellers, whose part in the war was very much that of victims. They shared what little food they had with Fred and André, mostly bread and dry sausage. Like homeless people, they were supported by the charity of strangers.

As if the situation wasn't bad enough, I was kept awake

each night by nightmares, reminding me of the incident on the road to Aachen. In some, the tables were turned and my German guard slipped his knife into my belly. I saw my mother's face, crying over the flag-draped coffin.

The German men in the shelter were very cautious about what they said to the two strangers. One short, bald-headed man, Herr Kohl, who sported a gray Hitleresque mustache, must have been the Nazi block warden, though he never admitted it. He never greeted anyone with a good morning or hello, but always "Heil Hitler." Whenever he came near, the other men would surreptitiously put a finger to their lips in warning. He secretly questioned the other residents about who Fred and André were, but he never approached them directly. Had he known their true identity, he would surely have wanted to turn them in, but to do so under the current circumstances would have been impossible. The end of Nazi control was near for Aachen.

On the second morning, as they two joined their cohabitants in the shelter for a meager breakfast, one of the women who had never spoken much spoke directly to Fred.

"How close are the Americans?" she asked. "Do you think they will come here?"

Fred just shrugged. "How would I know?" he asked her.

"I'm so terribly worried," she continued. "Surely you've heard the radio broadcasts about how brutal they are — how they have a free hand to rape the German women and treat us like slaves."

One of the men, an elderly gentleman spoke up: "You

can't believe everything you hear, Marta."

"He's right," Fred said.

The elder gentleman said, "For my part, I hope they come soon and end this misery we've had to live under for too many years."

One of the men in the group suddenly put a finger to his mouth. Kohl pushed his way into the center of the circle.

"Guten morgen, Herr Kohl."

"Heil Hitler!"

Kohl stared at Fred and André for a moment. Fred nodded at him; André just smiled. Suddenly, Kohl seemed uncomfortable in their presence and moved away without a word.

By late afternoon that day, the fighting on the street above had escalated tremendously. In his lousy German, André told Fred he wanted to go outside and take a look.

"Are you crazy?" Fred asked. The sound of artillery and machine gun fire had been going on uninterrupted for nearly two hours. André did not understand the word crazy and said, "What?" several times. Fred finally held a hand in front of his nose and pretended to sneeze. "Nuts!"

André grinned, understanding at last, and patted Fred reassuringly on the shoulder. "I'll be fine," he said, and started for the stairway to go out. Before he got there, Mr. Kohl stepped in front of him.

"You can't go out there," the little man said.

André towered over him like a giant over a dwarf. For a moment it seemed as if he would knock Kohl out of his way, but instead he smiled and said in French, "I just want a little air, it's very stuffy in here." Then he walked around Kohl and disappeared up the stairs.

For a little while, I figured I'd never see my partner again. Minutes passed. The gunfire above continued unabated. I was getting ready to go after him, when the sound of the door slamming shut at the top of the stairs signaled André's return. Everyone, including Kohl, quickly gathered around him to ask him what was happening out there.

"The fireworks are still coming from both directions," André said. "To me that means that the Americans are at least on the outskirts, if not already in the city. The German troops must be retreating, because I didn't see a single soldier or anyone else on the street."

The mood in the little basement shelter changed suddenly.

The older men became very outspoken about their leadership. The women were much more subdued. Marta shrunk into a corner alone still thinking about the propaganda she had heard. Other women spoke of their husbands and sons who were somewhere out there fighting what appeared now to be a lost cause.

The most outspoken of all was the elderly man who had tried to comfort Marta. He was with her in the corner, his arm around her shoulders, when suddenly he called out to Mr. Kohl: "For all this you can thank your Fuehrer. Just look at what he has done for us!"

Kohl was speechless.

They heard the rumble of heavy vehicles on the street above. Tanks and trucks were moving through the city. It was the 26th U.S. Infantry Regiment of the First Infantry Division.

Fred spoke up: "I think it's time that someone goes upstairs bearing a white flag. Perhaps Mr. Kohl would do the honors?"

Everyone in the room agreed. Kohl had no choice but to comply. As the group gathered to follow him up into the street, Fred took Marta aside. She had the look of a frightened child in her eyes.

"You have nothing to worry about," Fred reassured her. "My friend and I are American agents. Our soldiers will not hurt you, I guarantee it. We are civilized people."

On the street, American tanks and trucks were rolling. The group found itself standing among people from other buildings who had emerged blinking at the daylight, as they had, from cellars and bomb shelters nearby. Fred and André thrilled to the sight of the military parade, but the people around them were the vanquished, not the victors, and the mood was subdued. André caught sight of Kohl standing toward the back of the group and went over to him and inquired. "That little insignia you were wearing the last couple of days, where is it?"

Kohl looked bewildered. Apparently he could not understand André's torturous use of the German language. I stepped in to translate. Kohl pointed to his pocket. He had quietly removed the swastika before leaving the basement.

"Give it to me now, you little Nazi bastard," André growled. "I want to have something to remember you by."

Fred translated and, like a man in shock, Kohl reached into his pocket and handed over what had once been a symbol of pride to him. André took it and turned his back on the little man without another word.

The First Infantry Division that entered Aachen that day was one of America's crack units in World War II. It played a pivotal role in the liberation of Europe. By the end of the war, this division alone would sustain more than 1,500 fatalities and more than 1,500 wounded, of which another 600 eventually died of their wounds.[10]

---

[10] The 1st Infantry Division, known as the "Big Red One" because of its insignia, entered combat in 1942 as part of the invasion of North Africa. After the German "Afrika Korps" surrender in 1943, the division moved on to take Sicily, quickly overpowering the Italian defenses. By the spring of 1944, the 1st Infantry Division transferred to England to begin preparations for the Invasion of Normandy. On D-Day, June 6, 1944, the Big Red One stormed ashore at Omaha Beach. After the beachhead was secured, the Division moved on to liberate Liege, Belgium, and pushed to the German border, crossing through the fortified Siegfried line. The division attacked the first major German city, Aachen. After many days of bitter house-to house fighting, the German commander surrendered the city on Oct. 21, 1944. The division pushed into Germany, crossing the Rhine River engaged in a massive counterattack in the Ardennes sector, known as the Battle of the Bulge. The Big Red One was fighting in Czechoslovakia when WW2 in Europe ended in May.

Chapter Six

With Aachen now in Allied hands, it was time for André and Fred to return to the safe house in Luxembourg. The trip back through territory solidly in Allied hands was uneventful. They saw many vehicles returning from the front lines filled with German prisoners of war. Other trucks and tanks were headed in the opposite direction, toward Germany.

As soon as we arrived at the safe house, we received a message that an officer was on his way to our post with a young French woman who claimed to be an American agent. She was being sent to us for verification since G-2 had no knowledge of her. No name was included in the message, so we had no idea if, in fact, it was one of our people.

The two men spent the afternoon and early evening recuperating from their days spent in the cramped basement in

Aachen. At about 10 p.m., an army command car arrived at the house. From the front door, Fred watched an infantry captain emerge from the backseat and then hold out his hand to help Colette out after him. She straightened her dress, and then brushed back a stray lock of black hair before looking up and seeing Fred.

She ran up and we embraced. I kissed her, and then held her at arm's length to look at her. Then I noticed the streaks of dirt across her face and her limp unwashed hair. She was clearly exhausted.

"Fred, I'm so happy to see you," she said, kissing him again on the lips. Then she stepped back, "Look at me, I'm disgusting. I haven't eaten in two days, and I haven't bathed in three."

The officer was standing just behind Colette now. He said, "I told the young lady you would need to debrief her immediately."

Fred smiled at him. "Of course," he said. "But, we'll take it from here, Captain. You can go home to bed now."

The Captain hesitated but only for a moment and then he was gone, the command car leaving a smell of exhaust in its wake.

Colette looked at Fred. "May I take a bath and eat something before the debriefing?"

Fred laughed. "Of course you can, Colette. We'll take care of you now. The only problem is I don't believe we have any women's clothing here." He shrugged. "I'm certain we can find something suitable for you."

Colette's bath took more than an hour and a half. When she came out of the bathroom, she was wearing her new outfit – army fatigues with pants and sleeves at least eight inches too long.

We had prepared her a big dinner, and she ate like there was no tomorrow. It was obvious that she was very tired, so I told her to go to sleep and we would debrief her in the morning, after a good night's rest. No, she insisted on talking to me now.

Colette removed some papers from her small purse. They were folded over many times and while she carefully unfolded them, she explained that she had taken them from her colonel's briefcase just before she left him. "A courier delivered these papers to him less than an hour before I took them," she said, proudly.

Fred took one glance and knew that they were important. The documents outlined a German counteroffensive plan, indicating in detail exactly where and when an SS Division was being assembled northeast of the front. "How did you take them without him knowing?"

"After he read these, he told me he was tired and wanted to rest before meeting with his officers. I watched him place these papers in his briefcase and helped myself as soon as I was certain he was asleep. Then I got out of there in a hurry."

Fred was smiling on the inside but struggled to maintain a serious expression. André, on the other hand, who had been listening intently to the debriefing, was visibly impressed.

"I told you she was something special," Fred said. André just raised his bushy eyebrows, which Fred had noted were already turning grey.

The next morning, while Colette was still sleeping, a major from Corps came to see Fred. He said Intelligence had suspected that the Germans were planning a counteroffensive, but the information we had given them had made all the difference.

"Up until last night, we didn't know where or how hard to hit them," the Major said. "Those documents you provided answered all our questions. We've launched a combined Army-Air Force operation." He paused to light a cigarette and then said, "It will squash their counteroffensive before it even gets started. I'd like to thank your agent personally, but I've got to get moving. Where is he?"

Fred grinned. "She is still asleep, Major. Don't worry, though, we'll thank her for you."

The Major shook Fred's hand. "You know," he said, "We used to make jokes about OSS."

"Yes, I know – Oh So Silly – right?" He shrugged. "I always preferred Oh So Secret, myself. The point is we didn't think we needed you guys," he glanced toward the stairway to the bedrooms, "and gals. We were wrong."

When Colette finally came out of her room, it was nearly noon. André cooked her a breakfast of eggs and bacon that she devoured with the same fervor as she had dinner the night before. She was still wearing the oversized Army fatigues, so Fred took her in the jeep to look for more suitable clothing in

Luxembourg City. At a small alteration shop, she picked out a couple of dresses and was soon transformed. The curves of her small body made heads turn on the sidewalk outside the shop. As they drove around the city, Colette was all radiant smiles, basking in the knowledge that she had succeeded in taking some measure of revenge on the Germans.

At a stop sign somewhere in the old city I spotted an American soldier I recognized. I pulled up to the curb and told Colette to wait for me there. "I need to speak to that guy over there," I told her. "Our mothers are close friends in Vineland, New Jersey." She just smiled at me and nodded. As I approached, the soldier stopped dead in his tracks. He stared at me, absolutely stunned. "Jack!" I said. "How the hell are you?"

Jack didn't say a word. He reached into his uniform breast pocket, pulled out a V-mail letter and handed it to Fred.
"What's this?"
"Read it."
The letter from Jack's mother began, *"Everyone was quite sad to get word that Mrs. Rosenfeld's son Fred has been killed. Frieda has been in mourning now for a week, since learning he was missing in action, presumed dead."*
"When did you get this?"
"Two days ago."

Colette and I hurried back to the house. By the time we got there, I had explained the situation and told her I would be leaving for Paris immediately. There at least I could attempt to make a phone call to my mother in New Jersey.

"Take me with you to Paris, Fred," Colette begged. "I have a sister there. She has a nice family and could help me get a new start. I don't want to return to my former life."

"I'll talk to André," Fred said. "We'll help you in any way we can."

At the house, Fred told André about his encounter with Jack. "I'm leaving for Paris immediately." André nodded in agreement. "And I'm taking Colette with me," Fred continued.

André nodded again. "There's really nothing more she can do for us now," he said. "Her colonel is certainly aware of what she did. But we've got to finish the debriefing and make a full report to our colonel, Fred. Before you go, let's talk to her and I'll write it up so you two can get on your way."

Colette came down from her room, with her few things packed. We sat around the small kitchen table as she finished her story.

"After I grabbed the papers out of his briefcase, I just walked out the front door of the house we were living in. The colonel's driver was sitting in the car. I told him I'd be back shortly; in case the colonel was looking for me. I said I needed to get some nice stockings. Then I walked away slowly, as if I was going for a stroll to the local shops. When I passed the colonel's headquarters, several of his officers were already standing in front. They all knew me and waved at me. There was a bicycle leaning up against the building, so I asked them who it belonged to. One of the officers told me it belonged to a

161

woman who worked inside as a maid. He said if I wanted it, I could just take it. So I did. And they all laughed as I rode off. Every time I passed some German soldiers, I would wave or throw kisses at them. No one tried to stop me.

"The further away I got, the lonelier and more frightened I became. I didn't stay on the main road, but took side roads and cut across fields. I was heading west, using the little compass you gave me, Fred. At one point two soldiers saw me and started shouting at me to stop. I thought this was it but they only wanted to warn me not to ride through the fields because they were filled with land mines. I thanked them and they suggested I join them since we seemed to be heading in the same direction. They were older men and I had the impression they were running away to the American lines just like me. They spoke very little, but when they did it was to complain about the war. I finally asked them where they were going, and they said they had lost their company and were trying to locate it, but they had to be very careful because if they were stopped by other troops, it might look like they were trying to desert. "I told them I was looking for my little sister, that we had been separated during the bombing. Just then we heard small arms fire nearby. It was getting dark. One of the soldiers said we were getting into a danger zone now, where we might meet up with German or Allied patrols at any time. He suggested we find shelter for the night. His friend said, 'Little lady, you don't have to be afraid of us. We're both old men and have grandkids your age.'

"After a while we came upon a small farmhouse, badly damaged and empty. We went inside and looked for food without any luck. Then we made ourselves as comfortable as we could and tried to sleep. Before long the two of them were snoring, but I couldn't sleep at all. I kept imagining what would happen if the German Military Police found us. I was certain my Colonel would be hot on my trail by now. I felt sorry for the old men and thought that if we were caught, I would say that they had taken me prisoner when they found me fleeing with the top secret documents. They at least would be heroes instead of being shot as deserters by the Nazi bastards. Instead, just before dawn I heard people approaching and a voice speaking in plain English, saying, check out that old building. I didn't know if they were Americans or Brits, but I got up and started yelling as loud as I could in both English and French.

"That woke the two Germans up. Their faces were as white as bed sheets when two American soldiers entered our hideout. The Americans took us to their company commanding officer, and from there I was put on a truck heading back to France. The two old soldiers went on another truck with other prisoners. The last I saw them, they looked relieved, even happy. As we drove, I had no idea where we were, but with every mile that passed I felt safer. Eventually a lieutenant sat down next to me and began to question me in French. I told him I needed to speak with an Intelligence officer. 'That's me,' he said. 'I'm the Assistant Division Intelligence Officer. What do you have to say?' I told him I was a French agent, working for the OSS, and that I needed to get to this safe house in Luxemburg. He went to get his captain, and I repeated my request. They seemed a bit dubious at first, but after I let them see the documents I was carrying, the captain ordered his assistant to take me where I wanted to go. The rest you know."

We sat in silence for moment as André finished writing in his notebook. He looked up and said, "That's very fine, you've done quite well, Colette. You've made us and your country proud."

"Are we going to Paris now?" Colette asked. I stood up. "Yes, immediately."

André walked them to the jeep. "I'll write the report and stay in touch with HQ for the next two days and then I'll join you in Paris, Fred. Be sure to report to Colonel Bruce and bring him up to date."

"I will," Fred said, jumping into the jeep. He was already pulling away, when André shouted out, "Good luck making the phone call to your mother!"

To say I was preoccupied as I drove to Paris would be a grand understatement. I drove as fast as the jeep would go and the road would allow me. We wove in and out of slow moving truck traffic heading to Paris. With the windshield down, conversation with Colette was nearly impossible. I looked at her from time to time; she wore a very contented smile and seemed undisturbed by my reckless driving. I had never seen her so happy.

They arrived in Paris after 11 p.m. Colette directed Fred

to her sister's house in a quaint neighborhood near the river. Fred was in a hurry to get to OSS Headquarters, but Colette insisted on a very long good-bye. Finally, he pushed her away. "It's getting late. I have to go on. Go in the house and make certain that your sister is there. I'll wait here until you are inside."

"Fred, come with me, I'd like you to meet my family."

"I have to go," Fred said, firmly. "In a few days, you, your family and André and I will celebrate together."

She finally went to the door and rang the bell several times. A moment later her sister and brother-in-law appeared in the doorway and threw their arms around her. For a moment, Fred watched, happy to see Colette in the arms of her family. In his heart he knew he might never see her again. But he also knew that what they had shared was something special that would stay with them both forever. Thinking of his own family far away in Vineland, Fred sped off toward headquarters.

Chapter Seven

Fred drove directly to headquarters and nearly forgot to shut the jeep off when he parked. It was after midnight and no one was there except the guards. They accepted his pass and let him go into a lieutenant's office. He knew he wasn't supposed to be doing what he was doing, but he didn't care. He picked up the phone and got the Washington OSS headquarters on the line. He told the operator to connect him to his mother and uncle's telephone number in Vineland, New Jersey.

"Is this a personal call?"

"You're damn right," Fred said.

"I'm sorry, sir, but we're not authorized to connect personal calls. Who is this?"

"Damn it, put me through, this is an emergency!"

"I can't do that without proper authority from the Administrative Officer."

"Put him on the phone then."

"Sir, it's after hours. The staff won't be in until the morning."

Fred was becoming more desperate with every passing second. "Listen, I'm sorry, what's your name?"

She told him her name was Ellen.

"Ellen, I've just come back from the front lines. It was pretty bad there, but I made it, only to hear that some idiot reported me missing in action to my mother. All I want to do is to let the poor old woman know that her only son is still alive. Is that too much to ask, Ellen?"

She softened a bit. "You're really not even authorized to call this office, let alone make a private call. It's strictly forbidden. But, I'll tell you what, I'm alone here now and if we keep it between you and me, I'll put you through for five minutes. You must be quick because I never know who might walk in here. Wild Bill himself sometimes comes in after hours."

"Ellen, Ellen, I really appreciate this," Fred said. "And I promise no one will ever know about this call except you, me and my mother."

The telephone in Frieda's little farmhouse in Vineland, New Jersey rang several times before her voice came across. The moment she heard Fred say, "Hello, Mother," she knew. "I can't believe it," she cried out. "Is it really you, Fred?"

"Yes," Fred assured her. "I'm not dead, mother. I'm in Paris."

Then my mother became nearly hysterical, sobbing and chanting over and over, "My boy is alive, my boy is alive." At some point Uncle Max must have come into the room with her, because she changed to "Our boy is alive!" But I still could not get her to stop. I had to talk over her chanting. I told her I would write to her that night and that she and Uncle Max should take care of themselves and not worry any more about me. I told her I would be coming home someday soon.

It was difficult, but Fred had no choice but to say good-bye and hang up. Later his mother would tell him that she couldn't sleep all that night, and in the morning she didn't know if the call had been real or just a wishful dream until Uncle Max confirmed that it had happened. Then Frieda nearly convinced Max that they had both imagined Fred's call. It wasn't until his letter arrived a week later that their minds were put at ease.

Fred stayed on the telephone to thank Ellen. "Give me your last name," he begged her. "When I get to Washington, I'd like to take you out for a drink."

"Forget it," she said. "It's better if we just pretend this never happened. Just keep your mouth shut about it and don't try it again. That will be reward enough for me."

I stepped out onto the Champs Elysees, feeling like a man brought back from the dead. The brisk winter air was invigorating. I felt so good, I didn't even bother to stop at Mimi Pension for a drink. Instead, I found a billet nearby and slept like a baby.

At headquarters the next day, Fred found out that Colonel Bruce was in London and not expected back until the next morning. With no one to report to, Fred spent the morning talking to the officer in charge of billeting. He reassigned Fred to a nice apartment about three blocks from headquarters, where Fred showered and shaved at midday. Then he went to Mimi Pension.

Several familiar OSS faces greeted him when he arrived at the tiny basement establishment. An air of celebration permeated the room; everyone had a story to tell about their exploits and an opinion about how soon it would all be over. The afternoon stretched on into evening, and the drinks flowed freely until nearly 4 a.m. Fred stumbled home and fell into bed just a couple of hours before he should have reported to headquarters. He slept soundly and didn't wake up until 10:30 a.m.

I rushed to the office, remembering how many times I had clashed with Colonel Bruce in the past and thinking that I had blown my moment of glory with him again.

Fred was waved directly in to Colonel Bruce's office. As he entered the room, the Colonel got up and came around his desk with arms outstretched and an uncharacteristic smile plastered on his face. "Fred," he greeted him, slapping him on the back and grabbing his hand to shake before Fred could finish his salute: "Superb job! Superb job!"

Word had already arrived from Army field headquarters. Guided by the information Colette had provided, the Air Force had destroyed the SS staging area. Army units had moved in, taking untold prisoners. The German counteroffensive was stopped dead in its tracks.

Fred left the Colonel's office elated. André was due in the next day; all was well with the world. He spent another evening with friends at the night club, but made it only as far as 10 p.m. before turning in. The next morning, André was standing outside Colonel Bruce's office smoking a cigarette. Fred was surprised to see how concerned Andre was about him.

"I was worried you raced back so fast and had an accident," he said. "Don't forget, I know all too well how you drive when you're in a hurry."

Fred couldn't believe he was hearing this from the man who had taught him that war was hell. Now, as the war winded down emotions were running high. There was still work to do, though. André was there to present the written report to Colonel Bruce, so Fred volunteered to turn in the jeep and other equipment. More than an hour later, after he had completed all the paperwork required to return equipment, he returned to the offices to look for André.

He checked first with the administrative officer, Captain Smith. "I've been looking for you, Fred," the Captain said when he walked in."

"I've been looking for my partner, André. Do you know where he is?"

"He's already come and gone," the Captain replied. "I'm not sure where he went, but I have your orders cut." He held up a sheaf of papers. "Colonel Bruce is very pleased with your performance. The information you got stopped the German counteroffensive cold. Excellent work. You're to be commended. Anyway, you need to get your things together and catch the next flight to London. Congratulations, Fred, you've been promoted to liaison officer."

I went to my billet, looking for André all the way. After packing my few clothes and other belongings into a duffel bag, I called the motor pool for a ride to the airport. I stood on the sidewalk, waiting for my car, smoking cigarettes and still expecting André to show his face.

But the OSS driver arrived shortly and, before I knew it, I was at the airport, standing by for the first available C-47 supply plane with an empty seat. I guess it was about then that I started to realize I was not going to see my partner again. Somehow, I sensed that this parting was forever.

In fact, I did not see André again until an OSS reunion in Washington in 1985, 41 years later. And then, several years later, when I started to put these events down on paper, I called his farm in Virginia from my home in Texas. His daughter answered and told me sadly that André was too far gone with Alzheimer's disease to talk with me. She assured me that she knew who I was and thanked me for the call. Shortly after, I heard that André had died. He was a brave and fearless man, and I will always remember him as a true friend.

PART THREE

Return to Nuremberg

Chapter One

In London again, Fred served as liaison officer between the Political Intelligence Division of the British Foreign Office and various American agencies, including the OSS and Military Intelligence. His office was located in Bush House in the Trafalgar Square area. In the same building, the BBC made their foreign broadcasts. Friendly German prisoners of war, who were kept at a special camp near Ascot, were brought to Bush House daily for broadcasts to Germany. They would tell their fellow countrymen what was really happening – in other words, just how badly Germany was losing the war.

The operation was a joint British-American affair. Great care was taken in bringing the prisoners from Ascot to London because anti-German sentiment was naturally very high. Some of the prisoners were the sons of pre-1933 opposition party officials; others were simply anti-Hitler. All of them were willing to cooperate with the Allies. In addition to their anti-

Hitler sentiments, many used the opportunity to let their families back home know that they were alive and well.

The Germans were dressed in civilian clothes and driven to London in the company of an American sergeant in an ordinary looking station wagon. For security reasons, the local police between Ascot and London were notified in advance that this particular vehicle carried a special contingent of German POWs. They were told to keep this information strictly confidential.

In case of an accident, strict procedures were to be followed and the proper authorities, including Fred, were to be notified. The prisoners could not be allowed to infiltrate the local population no matter how sympathetic they were to the Allied cause. It was a matter of public trust.

Early one foggy morning, an accident occurred along the road to London. Several cars were smashed, including the station wagon. People from the cars had been thrown onto the road. The first British police officer to approach the prisoner vehicle asked the American sergeant, "Ascot?" Clutching his injured leg, the burly American replied, "No, just a bad bruise on my thigh."

The day the war ended in Europe, I received constant telephone calls from Joyce. She wanted to know if it was time yet to raise the flag because everyone was hearing rumors that the war was over. By early afternoon, I was able to say yes. She came to Bush House immediately and we joined the throngs of people celebrating in the street. It was a celebration I shall never forget. Walking to Piccadilly

174

Circus, we saw a Chinese sailor hanging by one arm from the top of a lamppost, waving his nation's flag. On the street, people were embracing and kissing, whether they knew each other or not.

Joyce and Fred went to OSS headquarters to celebrate with old friends and colleagues. Mimi Pension was so packed with revelers it was impossible to get near the bar to buy a bottle. Someone went to the infirmary and broke out medicinal alcohol. They mixed it with grapefruit juice and toasted the war's end. The celebrations went on into the wee hours of the morning.

A couple of months before the war ended, Nuremberg was captured. I received a call from the commanding officer of OSS London. He knew I was born in Nuremberg and knew the city well. He asked me to go there and report on what facilities were available that were in good condition and suitable for use as a headquarters. I had no idea what the headquarters would be used for, I was simply delighted to take this trip back to the city of my birth.

Fred landed at the airport on a cold spring morning. A jeep with a driver was waiting for him. On the way into town, at a certain point, Fred ordered the driver to stop. The young soldier watched with a puzzled expression as Fred got out of the jeep and stood by the side of the road, staring at the site before him. Fred began to shake and soon was convulsed with laughter.

"What strikes you so funny, sir?" the driver asked.

"This may be hard for you to believe," Fred said, taking a deep breath to stop from laughing uncontrollably. "But I was born in this town and I know it well. And I know that it would have been absolutely impossible to look from this point clear across this old city because there used to be a mass of buildings in the way."

The soldier looked in the direction Fred was pointing and saw, as Fred did, nothing but empty lots strewn with rubble for as far as the eye could see. "Really?"

Fred nodded. "Our artillery certainly did its job well," he said, still grinning.

Perhaps I should have felt sorry for what had happened to what was once a great German city, but after what Nuremberg, the cradle of Nazi anti-Semitism, had done to my family, all I could feel was satisfaction at the job my new country's military had done.

The young driver took Fred to his billet in the Grand Hotel near the railway station. As a boy, Fred had never been inside this magnificent building since it had borne a large sign forbidding Jews to enter. He walked in now, feeling a rush of emotion.

The hotel appeared to have been spared the worst of the war. Its lobby was lit by an enormous crystal chandelier, and ornate artwork graced its walls. Fred received the keys to his room on the third floor, dropped his duffel bag there and went back out to walk the streets.

Naturally, the first places I wanted to see in Nuremberg were the houses where I was born and lived with my family for the first 16 years of my life – Heideloffplatz numbers 3 and 15. As I approached, I could see they had been heavily damaged by aerial bombardment and artillery fire. Staring up at the cracked windows of my old home, I remembered the many good times with my family around me. At that point I still had no idea how many of my close relatives had died at the hands of the Nazis. I thanked God that my mother and Uncle Max were safe at home on the farm in Vineland, and I turned my back on the old building as if I was walking away from the past once and for all. Walking on through the old city, I couldn't help but notice the stench of death. There were still many dead bodies buried beneath the rubble.

That night, Fred slept soundly in a luxurious queen-sized bed in his room at the Grand Hotel. He had been out late, exploring the city and had collapsed into bed without even turning on the lights. In the middle of the night, he woke needing to use the bathroom. He made his way across the darkened room, opened the bathroom door and was greeted by an odd orange light and a cool breeze. Squinting, he saw that the light came from a lamppost about 20 feet below. Had he taken another step forward, he would have wound up in Bahnhof Square. Apparently, the hotel had been the recipient of a direct hit, which had split the building in two. The desk clerk had failed to mention that Fred's room no longer offered the amenity of a bathroom.

For the next two days, Fred toured Nuremberg with his driver. They inspected hotels, former military billets, the city hall, school buildings and judicial buildings. In short, they visited all of the buildings that remained standing in the city, looking for a suitable headquarters for OSS. Some were already occupied by U.S. military personnel. Many were damaged, some more heavily than others.

"It seems we may have done too good of a job destroying this place," Fred mumbled, late on the second afternoon, as they drove away from a gutted school building.

"Where to next, sir?" asked the driver.

Fred thought for a moment. "Take me to the courthouse between Nuremberg and Furth," he said.

It was a short drive. When they arrived, the building looked too good to be true. They walked through the empty halls, marveling at how one building could have survived the war so well. "This is the place," Fred said, smiling, as they got back into the jeep. Indeed, the building would eventually become headquarters for the International Military Tribunal.

Chapter Two

General Donovan was appointed associate chief prosecutor of the International Military Tribunal at Nuremberg in July 1945.[11] Fred and several other OSS members working in London received orders to report to the city. Before leaving, he spent a last evening on the town with Joyce. They went dancing at the same little club where they had met.

Fred returned to Nuremberg aboard a C-47 and was assigned to work for the U.S. prosecution staff. He served as an

---

[11] The October 1943 Moscow Declaration, signed by President Franklin D. Roosevelt, British Prime Minister Winston Churchill and Soviet leader Josef Stalin, stated that at the time of an armistice persons deemed responsible for war crimes would be sent back to the countries where the crimes had been committed and judged according to the laws of the nation concerned.

Major war criminals, whose crimes could be assigned no particular geographic location, would be punished by joint decisions of the Allied governments. The trials of leading German officials before the International Military Tribunal (IMT), the best known of the postwar war crimes trials, formally opened in Nuremberg, Germany, on November 20, 1945, only six and a half months after Germany surrendered.

interrogator, making use of his German language skills, in preparation for the forthcoming trials of major German war criminals. They were all there, Heinrich Himmler, Hermann Göring, etc. In the beginning, Fred conducted the interrogations accompanied by different prosecutors. Eventually, he conducted them alone.

> *As more and more documents were discovered, it became easier and easier to interrogate the bastards because we had written evidence of their activities. On top of that, we were finding more witnesses, both voluntary and involuntary. One of my first interrogations stands out in my mind, that of Hermann Göring himself.*

Chief prosecutor Robert Jackson called Fred into his office on a Wednesday afternoon. "Listen, Fred, we need Göring to corroborate some information and he hasn't been very cooperative thus far. I want you to read this file over carefully and start working with him immediately. As you'll see, all we need is a simple answer, yes or no. But we need it before Friday. I've seen you work and I think you can handle it."[12]

---

[12] Hermann Göring was the highest-ranking Nazi official tried at Nuremberg. After Hitler's appointment as chancellor of Germany in 1933, Göring took on many positions of power and leadership within the Nazi state, including commander in chief of the *Luftwaffe* (German Air Force) and, at the outbreak of war in Europe, Hitler's acknowledged successor. It was Göring who ordered a "total solution" to the "Jewish question." The International Military Tribunal charged Göring on all four counts: crimes against peace; war crimes; crimes against humanity; and conspiracy to commit crimes against peace, war crimes and crimes against humanity.

Fred hoped the boss was right. Göring had quickly developed a reputation around the office for being both arrogantly uncooperative and disarmingly charismatic. Even some of the hard-nosed military police who guarded him were reduced to schoolboy awe in his presence.

All interrogations were conducted in special rooms that consisted of a small table with three chairs around it, one for the interrogator, one for the person being interrogated and one for the court reporter, who took down a transcript of everything that was said on her special machine. There were two armed guards in the room at all times. Under the desk near the interrogator's seat was an alarm button that would call additional guards into the room in case of trouble. One guard stood directly behind the interrogee at all times. On the desk was a file tray. In it was a hidden microphone connected to a tape recorder in an upstairs room. Behind the interrogator was a window looking out over the prison yard and the prison beyond.

Fred began his interrogation of Göring on Thursday morning at eight, just minutes after the prisoners had finished their breakfast. He had little trouble getting the big man to answer his first basic questions such as name, rank and serial number. After that, however, Göring's attention appeared to wander. He asked Fred to repeat questions, made side comments to the guards and the court reporter about what a marvelous day it was outside and how unfortunate it was for all of them to be cooped up inside.

Fred felt his stomach begin to churn. He stared at Göring, who stared back contemptuously. Long silences were broken only by the sound of birds singing outside and the wooden chairs creaking as they shifted their weight. Göring knew exactly what Fred wanted to hear and took great pains to circumvent the questions, asking questions of his own. "How is it you don't know where I was on that day? It should be right there in your file."

"Just answer my question." Fred replied, feeling his ears burning.

Eventually, they heard the sound of the lunch bell. Göring began to rise, saying he was returning to the prison for lunch.

"Sit down!" Fred snapped. "The interrogation is over when I say so."

"I refuse to answer any more questions," Göring said. "It's lunchtime."

"That is your prerogative," Fred replied. "I don't mind waiting until you're ready to talk, but in the meantime, we'll just sit here."

I lit a cigarette, moving as slowly as I could to keep from shaking. Göring was glaring at me, so as I exhaled, I glared right back. In my mind, I thought of all my people — relatives, friends and neighbors — people I knew and people I did not know, who had suffered and died because of the actions of this man and his cohorts. This particular interrogation was of minor consequence. It was so inconsequential today I cannot recall the exact details of

182

what it was all about. But to me, it was perhaps the most important moment of my life. Normally, I would have offered the prisoner a cigarette to put him at ease. This time I did not. Upon the ringing of the second bell, signaling the end of lunchtime when all prisoners were required to return to their cells, I announced that the interrogation was over.

"You may return to your cell now, Herr Göring," Fred said with a smile.

As the guards escorted the former *Reichsmarshall* out of the interrogation room, Fred noted how baggy his pants were becoming. Prison food was not quite as rich as the food Göring was used to, and now he had missed one lunch altogether.

That afternoon, Fred had Göring brought back into the same room and again they followed the same procedure. The prisoner was willing to answer basic questions only and fell silent when Fred probed him about the more important topic at hand. When the bell went off for dinner, Göring said he would talk no longer. Fred shrugged and they sat facing each other until the second bell. Again, Fred smoked a cigarette. Again, the two men glared at each other through the haze of smoke.

Before leaving his office for the evening, following normal procedure, Fred put in a request to interrogate Göring before breakfast early the next morning.

Göring entered the interrogation room with a scowl on his face. Before even sitting down, he said, "The answer to your question is yes."

Fred opened his file, removed his list of questions and

placed it on the table in front of him. "Sit down, Herr Göring," he said. "We must start from the beginning." He reached under the desk and flipped the switch for the tape recorder.

When the bell rang for breakfast, Göring was still talking. Fred held up his hand. "That'll be enough. You may go to breakfast now."

The guard led Göring back to the prison for his first meal in 24 hours.

During those early days, many of the prisoners were, like Göring, belligerent and uncooperative. Others looked for ways to ingratiate themselves to their former enemies, hoping to gain leniency. Fred grew more and more angry as the days passed and he realized that these men, who had shown no mercy when they were in power, were being treated with a certain amount of dignity under international law.

Another early interrogation stands out in my mind. It was of the SS and police leader in charge of the Nuremberg *area. He was a prisoner, not yet on trial himself, but being deposed as an involuntary witness for the prosecution. Listening to him rattle on in his Nuremberg dialect, I forgot myself, and my questions to him came out in the same local speech pattern.*

At one point, he grinned and said to me, "Listening to you, you sound like you come from Nuremberg." I could see that he wanted us to have something in common, so I answered, "That's right, I do come from Nuremberg. I'm one of the Jews you missed killing, but I am well aware of your past activities and I won't forget them for a minute."

Those first few months at the war crime trials were very difficult for Fred. There he was, in front of all those men and some women, whose aim had been to destroy him and all the rest of the Jews. And, worst of all, he realized that they had once had the power to do it.

Yet I had to learn to treat them as humanely as possible, knowing they would have never treated me so had the roles been reversed. Like all the other U.S. personnel, I realized that as Americans we were not like the Nazis. We had to show them, the rest of the Germans, as well as the rest of the world, that our way was the right way. This was a strict policy followed by all members of the prosecution staff throughout all the trials. Listening to all the evidence, especially during the medical experiments case, was most disturbing for us. Some of these witnesses went into great detail about how they killed people. In the beginning, I had trouble sleeping at night, lying in bed, reliving all the interrogations. After a while, I got used to it and it didn't bother my sleep any longer. I guess it's like a medical doctor whose first operation may be tough, but then he gets used to the sight of blood, and it doesn't bother him anymore.

Chapter Three

When General Donovan decided to return to the U.S., he asked, "Any of my boys want to go with me?"

The first trials were still weeks, if not months, away. Questions of protocol and the coordination of judicial teams from the United States and Russia were causing interminable delays in the process. Fred was as frustrated as anyone there and ready to take up the general's offer to go back home. He had been away for more than two years and yearned to see his mother and Uncle Max again. Within days, Fred's orders were cut and he boarded a liberty ship to return to the U.S. and receive his honorable discharge from the Army.

The trip across the Atlantic seemed longer than I remembered from my previous ocean voyages. Upon arriving, I had to report to OSS headquarters in Washington. I remember looking for the operator, Ellen, but by this time OSS was being disbanded and the new Strategic Service Unit (SSU) had new staff at nearly every position. I suffered through a week of confusion over whose jurisdiction I was under since all military personnel were on loan to the OSS. On October 8, 1946, I was finally given my discharge and made my way home to Vineland where I saw my mother and uncle for the first time in nearly three years.

Fred had called home from the port when his shipped first arrived in New York. There was only one public phone, and he had to stand in a long line to make the call. The line was just as long behind him when his turn finally came. It had been a familiar conversation with Frieda. "Mom, I'm in New York!" Frieda heard his voice and started crying with joy. "My boy is home," she chanted over and over again until the operator cut in to tell Fred his three minutes were up.

We were given passes to go the city since we wouldn't leave for Washington until the next day. I went to visit my cousins Irma and Adolf at 617 West End Avenue in Manhattan. When I rang the bell, their daughter Margot answered the door. She saw me and shouted, "Oh my God, it's Rudy!" She had mistaken me for our cousin Rudy Mannheimer, who was in the Navy.

Margot threw her arms around Fred and proceeded to tell him that her mother, Irma, was in the hospital.

"I want to go see her," Fred said.

"Just wait until Dad gets home," Margot said. "He'll take you."

Fred took the opportunity to call his mother again from his cousins' house. This time they managed to have a lengthy conversation.

"When are you coming home?" Frieda asked.

"I've got to go to Washington and apply for my discharge," Fred answered. "It shouldn't be long, Mama."

I had no idea then what a hassle it would be to get discharged. Once in Washington, it took more than a week, traveling back and forth between the State Department and the War Department. When I went to the War Department, they told me that OSS had been transferred to the State Department, and they could not release me without State Department approval. When I went to the State Department, they said I was under Army jurisdiction, and they could not release me either. I was thinking about just packing my bag and going home, when I received orders to report to Fort Monmouth, New Jersey, where after several more days, I received my discharge.

Fred returned to Vineland and enjoyed two weeks of rest and relaxation with Frieda and Uncle Max before he started looking for a job. He saw several of his old girlfriends, all of whom seemed flighty and foolish compared with Joyce and, of course, Colette.

One night at dinner, Fred told his mother and uncle the story of Colette, leaving out some of the more personal details.

They listened in awe. That same night, Frieda asked Fred if he enjoyed the eggs and sausage she had sent him. Fred burst out laughing.

"What's so funny?" Frieda asked.

I had almost forgotten the story of the package that followed me throughout Europe. My mother had sent a dozen hard-boiled eggs, dipped in paraffin to keep them fresh, and one of her homemade sausages to me while I was still working in the Morale Operations office in London. The package arrived one day after I had left for Paris so it was forwarded to my new Paris address.

Military mail moved slowly in those days. I imagine it sat at the airport for weeks before being placed on a C-47 for Paris. By the time it arrived, André and I were at work in Nancy. Once again, the package was forwarded to my new address, and once again, by the time it arrived, I had moved on. I could have used that food, during the siege of Aachen while we waited out the battle in the apartment dwellers' basement. Instead it waited for me back in Nancy, where I never returned.

Eventually, some bright mail clerk sent it back to Paris where I had just boarded a plane for London. Captain Smith forwarded the now tattered package back to London. On a hot summer day in 1946, I received a call from the local military post office. "Is this Fred Rodell? We've got a package waiting for you here, but don't bother coming to the front door, pal. You'll find it outside the back door. It stinks to high heaven!" My mother's precious eggs and sausage had traveled the same route through Europe as I had, only to go bad.

Uncle Max tried again to convince Fred to stay on the farm and work with the chickens, but to no avail. Vineland was too small a town for Fred Rodell. Two weeks and two days after returning home, he took the train to New York to look for work. While visiting his cousin Adolf at his place of business on Wall Street, he ran into General Donovan on the street by pure coincidence. Fred almost didn't recognize Wild Bill in his civilian clothes.

"Good to see you, son," the general said, shaking Fred's hand. "Come on up to my office where we can have a good talk."

The general's law offices occupied several floors of a building at No. 2 Wall Street. Fred followed him into the reception area; the general told one of the secretaries to hold all calls. He put his hand on Fred's shoulder and said, "I want to have a good long talk with one of my boys."

The young secretary smiled at Fred as he walked by. Inside the general's office, Fred was duly amazed at the mahogany furnishings He sank into a comfortable chair in front of the general's desk and listened to him talk of how much he missed the old days. Eventually, he asked Fred what his plans were.

"I've been living at home in New Jersey," Fred said. "You know, taking some time to see my family again."

The general nodded his approval.

"But there isn't much to do on a farm in Vineland," Fred said, shrugging. "I've come to New York to look for a job."

"Son, a young man with your experience and qualifications should be working for our government."

"The way I see it, to work for the government, who you know is more important than what you know," Fred said.

The general laughed. "You've got a point there, Fred. But you know me. Give me a phone number where I can reach you. I'll make some calls to Washington, set up some appointments for you, and call you tomorrow to tell you who to contact."

Bright and early the next morning, the telephone rang in the little farmhouse in Vineland, New Jersey. It was General Donovan calling to tell Fred he had an appointment the next day with Secretary of State Edward Stettinius. "He'll see you at the State Department as soon as you get there," the general assured Fred.

I took the train to Washington the next day and went immediately to the State Department. Sure enough, I was escorted directly to Mr. Stettinius' office, where I waited for more than an hour to see him. When he came out, he greeted me, "So, you're one of General Donovan's boys. "He shook hands with me, smiled at me and that was the end of the meeting. However, before leaving, he dictated a recommendation for me to one of his aides, who promptly ushered me into another office, where I met a second assistant. I went through a series of these assistants, receiving a written recommendation from each one before the last one made a call to the White House and told me to report immediately to a military officer there.

Fred's head was spinning as he made his way to the White House. The military officer glanced briefly at the sheaf of recommendations Fred offered him and said, "How would you like to work for the U.S. military mission to the United Nations?"

"In New York?"

The officer nodded.

"Sounds good to me," Fred said.

"Go to the Pentagon immediately," he glanced at his watch. "It's getting late and those fellows won't stay a minute past five. I'll get you a car to take you over there fast."

While they waited for the car to arrive, the officer told Fred to report to Room 1707 at the Pentagon. He couldn't remember the name of the colonel Fred needed to see but he said, "I'll think of the name and call him before you get there so he'll be expecting you."

I arrived at the Pentagon twenty minutes before five and went directly to Room 1707. Sure enough, a colonel was sitting behind the desk. I handed over my stack of recommendations and he leafed through them.

"Fine," the colonel said. "I'll need you to fill out this application." He looked at his watch. "It's almost five, so I'll call downstairs and tell them to wait for you so you can get a medical examination. Report back to me here, when you're done and we'll get the ball rolling."

They rushed Fred through his medical examination and he was back in the Colonel's office just minutes before six.

"How does $7,000 a year to start sound?" The Colonel asked him.

"It sounds good," Fred replied.

"You'll be reviewed and receive a raise in three months if you do well."

"That's fine," said Fred.

"Very good, then. Sign here."

As Fred signed the paper work, the Colonel asked, "How soon can you be ready to go to Nuremberg?"

"Nuremberg? Oh, any time, any time at all," Fred answered, trying to make sense of the question.

"Very good, then, we'll get in touch with you soon."

The colonel followed me out of his office, putting on his coat and hat as he went, a good hour past his usual quitting time. I watched him get into a car and speed away. Standing on the steps of the Pentagon, I kept asking myself, "Nuremberg?" I found out later that the colonel I was supposed to see at the Pentagon had moved that morning into another office. Another colonel, who had absolutely no knowledge of me, had moved in. He happened to be hiring people to work on the International Military Tribunal, a job I had just come from less than a month before.

Fred returned to Manhattan and told General Donovan what had happened. The General doubled over with laughter. "That's just like the Pentagon," he said, "When they've got nothing better to do, they move from one office to another. If you want to get out of it, I'll get you out."

"No," Fred said. "I signed up now and the money is good. I'll go back to Nuremberg. After all, I won't need any job training."

In fact, $7,000 in 1946 was a lot of money. So I took the job. Later on in Nuremberg, I became good friends with the colonel who had hired me. His name was David Marcus, and his nickname was Mickey. I asked him how he could have hired me like that without knowing anything about me. He said, "You came with so many recommendations, I didn't dare not hire you."

Colonel Mickey Marcus became famous. He was a West Point graduate, a lawyer and Jewish. When the Arab-Israeli War started in 1948, the Israelis had no trained military commanders. They asked Colonel Marcus to come to Israel to become the commander of the Israeli troops around Jerusalem. He became, in fact, the defender of Jerusalem.

Along with his other well-known attributes, Colonel Marcus was known as a ladies' man. One night, he went on a date with a local girl. He drank too much that night and when he returned to his post, he was challenged by a guard. Mickey did not speak Hebrew and didn't understand a word the guard said. He was shot and killed trying to get back into his own base. Kirk Douglas starred in the movie *Cast a Giant Shadow* about Colonel Mickey Marcus. The Israelis erected a statue in his honor.

Chapter Four

I took another ocean voyage, eastbound again. It was a time of great rejoicing among these shipmates, mostly refugees from the war returning home.

Fred spent most of his time during the voyage reading on deck while cool ocean breezes ruffled his hair. In the evenings, over dinner, he met and flirted with one or two girls, but nothing much happened.

Back in his home town again, he was assigned a billet with another young man, Thomas Marshall, a lawyer who had recently arrived to join the prosecution team. By that time the main trial was nearing its conclusion. Seven of the top Nazi political bosses were sentenced to die by hanging: Hermann Göring, Heinrich Himmler, Joachim von Ribbentrop, Wilhelm Keitel, Alfred Jodl, Julius Streicher and Hans Frank.

Only Göring escaped the noose. On the night before he was to hang, an American guard, a young Army lieutenant named Jack "Tex" Wheelis, helped him commit suicide. Tex was in charge of the warders and escorted the field marshall to interrogations and visits with his relatives. He also had a key to the storage room where the prisoner's personal belongings were kept. It is thought that Wheelis retrieved the fatal cyanide tablet from among his confiscated possessions and brought it to Göring concealed in a pot of skin cream. Lt. Wheelis was never questioned after the suicide.

Tex had come to admire the man, who was larger than life even in captivity, despite all the treachery that had been revealed about him at the trials. Tex believed he had established a deep friendship with Göring. The charismatic former number two leader of the Third Reich was found dead in his single bed in the cramped and musty cell on the morning of the hangings.

At Nuremberg once again I was assigned to my old job with the prosecution. I continued to interrogate prisoners scheduled for trial, but in this case at the Subsequent Proceedings, I was given special permission, although I was not an attorney, to examine and cross examine in court. They did this because I had the distinct advantage over most of the attorneys who did not speak German.

In the Nuremberg court, questions were asked in English and then translated for the defendant or witness into German. Answers given in German were then translated into English so that the prosecutor could ask the next question. Fred could ask the question in English, listen to the answer in German and formulate his next question while they were translating the answer into English. Thus, during the trial he was always a step ahead.

Interrogations were much simpler. In the small interrogation rooms like the one where Fred had previously interrogated Hermann Göring, Fred was both judge and jury. Accompanied only by the court reporter and an armed guard, he could speak freely to the defendants in German and let the translations be done later on paper.

During the case against the Nazi medical establishment, Fred's role was to interrogate the doctors who had carried out Germany's euthanasia program. Among them was Victor Brack, who steadfastly denied responsibility along with the others.

Still young and believing he was invincible, Brack approached the interrogations as if he was holding court himself. He answered Fred's questions as if he was dictating to a secretary and turned them into opportunities for discourse. Leaning forward, with legs crossed almost demurely, a cigarette dangling from his fingertips, Brack spoke matter-of-factly about the medical "contradictions" created by war. "We had to do things that would otherwise seem unnecessary," he said. But throughout more than a week in the little room with the court reporter clicking away on her little machine, he maintained he knew nothing about the brutal sterilization program that crippled and killed Jewish men and women.

He was a coarse peasant whom Hitler's whim had exalted into power. Like many of his sort in Nuremberg, he knew that it was all over, that Nazism and Germany had been

198

annihilated. Nevertheless, he kept on lying like all the others. He never showed the least sign of remorse, never seemed to be aware of the horrors he had committed. This perverted attitude was what abhorred me the most. The memory of this man still weighs heavily on my conscience although I know he was a butcher.

It was warm in the interrogation room on that morning. Brack had unbuttoned the top button of his uniform, a cigarette dangled from his fingertips. Fred handed him a blank sheet of paper.

"Mr. Brack, here is a piece of white paper, affix your normal signature," he commanded.

Brack hesitated before signing with a flourish. The court reporter noted his action: "The witness signs the paper."

Fred glanced at Brack's signature, then removed another document from his briefcase and laid it before him next to the blank sheet with his signature. The document, CINFO No. 5 was covered except for the signature at the bottom.

"Which of these two signatures is yours?" Fred asked.

Brack looked down at the two pieces of paper and shrugged. "Mr. Rodell," he said, "both of these two signatures are of course mine. The one on this document I recognize without any doubt as my signature."

Fred felt like slapping the man. Instead he simply said, "Victor Brack, our cat and mouse game is now over." He uncovered the top of the document. "Read this bloody document. It is a damn criminal letter that you wrote and probably forgot to burn in 1945."

The letter was from Brack to an underling, instructing him to begin a particularly brutal new method of sterilizing young Jewish women. Brack saw it immediately and the court reporter took note of his reaction: "The witness breaks down crying."

"I am absolutely unimpressed to see the SS general, who for years bathed his hands in blood, first lying so arrogantly and then breaking down crying," Fred said for the record. He paused long enough to light a cigarette of his own, his hands steady. Brack, still crying, was trying to light one cigarette from the butt of another, but his hands were trembling so violently he couldn't accomplish even this simple action.

"You should have thought of your criminal deeds before," Fred continued. "In your case, they started prior to 1933. If you had thought of them then, as you think of them now, you would not be sitting here in front of me as such a ridiculous creature."

Brack was whimpering now, like a child seeking comfort from his angry parent.

"I find it a little difficult to have compassion for one of the former leaders of greater Germany, who laughingly would watch while heads were rolling."

"Herr Doctor, Herr Doctor, I know I lied to you, but I will tell you everything, the full truth really. But please do not leave my lies in the protocol. Strike the whole interrogation in which I lied. I will now tell you the truth fully, everything."

Fred knew better. He took a long drag on his cigarette and blew the smoke in Brack's direction in a long, drawn out exhale. A small cloud of bluish smoke hung above the interrogation table.

"Well, Brack, I'm ready to begin a new interrogation now, but whether I will strike the interrogations with your lies – in which you are guilty of perjury – I will decide after I'm satisfied that you have answered my questions truthfully." Brack was nodding his head vigorously.

"Now I'm giving you your last opportunity to tell the truth," Fred began, deftly squashing out his cigarette in an overflowing ashtray on the table. "Before I do, I want to point out to you that it is to your advantage to be truthful. You may have noticed that it's not just your answers that we're depending on. Much of the information comes to us through our files and records that the gentlemen SS leaders forgot to destroy. If you tell the truth, and I mean the full truth, I have no reason to keep your lying declarations."

Just looking at Brack's pale face now made Fred's stomach turn, and he felt close to vomiting right there in front of the witness, court reporter and guard. Instead, he said, "I think you would also feel morally better if you tell us how things really were."

Brack looked up at him now, eyes narrowed. "Will I be indicted?"

"That I don't know. I'm only interested in your statements. We want to know what really happened during the Third Reich. Have you received an indictment?"

Brack shook his head and responded, "No."

"In that case, I can only recommend that you stick to the truth. Let's start the new interrogation now."

Brack sat back in his chair as if preparing himself. Fred

placed both hands on the edge of the table and spoke.

> *"What is your full name?"*
> "Victor Brack." "
> *"Are you the same Victor Brack whom I have interrogated very often?"*
> "Yes."
> *"Are you aware that you are still under oath?"*
> "Yes."

> *"Mr. Brack, since the day before yesterday, I have interrogated you exactly four times. In each of these interrogations I have had only one question for you which was: What do you know about the sterilization program for the Jews? So, I'm going to ask you once again. What do you know about the sterilization program of the Jews?"*

"Mr. Prosecutor Rodell, my answer is still the same. I know nothing, absolutely nothing about any sterilization."

Fred was not surprised. The court reporter did not react. The guard behind Brack stared straight ahead.

"Brack, you are not a jurist, but I think you know what perjury is? Brack nodded. "Yes of course."

"Very well, then let me put you under oath once again in case you forget the oath you gave before. Stand up, lift your right hand and repeat after me: 'I swear by God the Almighty that I will tell the full truth withholding nothing, so help me God.'"

Brack repeated the oath, and the court reporter duly took note.

Fred looked directly into Brack's ice blue eyes. "You realize that the withholding of facts in your statement is as much a violation of your oath as false statements under oath?

"Yes," Brack nodded again. "Yes, I do."

"Brack, what do you know about the sterilization program of the Jews?

"Nothing, absolutely nothing."

The new interrogation ended then. It was the last that Fred would hold with Brack. Later, after the court's indictment was handed down, Brack sought Fred out and asked for his support. Fred was incredulous and walked away from the man shaking his head.

He had not realized that although we had been forced to see each other so often, we were enemies. I don't think it was pure folly. On the contrary, all of Hitler's commanders were like that: dull-minded idiots. I'll never forget the look on his face in the courtroom, on the day Brack was sentenced to die by hanging. He looked as if he couldn't believe it.

And still later, when in the desperate attempt to find a reason for that woeful, uninspired depravity I asked him to tell me who had ever bestowed upon him the right to decide who could live and who had to die, he stared at me with his blurry eyes and answered, "But of course, I have been a member of the party since 1927." This is what the Reich's hangmen were: pale men, asking in peevish voices to see their wives.

Chapter Five

The Germans built for experimentation a special building, very narrow with nothing in it but a long counter.

SINFO #5 March 28, 1941: Victor Brack submitted to Himmler a report on the state of experiments in x-ray sterilization:

> One way to carry out these experiments in practice would be to have those people who are to be treated line up before a counter. There would be questions, and a form would be given to them to be filled out, the whole process taking two or three minutes.
>
> The official attendant, who sits behind the counter, can operate the apparatus in such a manner that he works a switch which will start both tubes together, as the rays have to come from both sides. Using one such

installation with two tubes, about 150 to 200 persons could be sterilized daily, while 20 installations could take care of about 3,000 to 4,000 persons daily.

In my opinion, the number of daily deportations will not exceed these figures. I estimate the cost of such installations to be between 20,000 and 30,000 marks per tube system; however, the cost of renovation of a building would have to be added to that as adequate safety measures for the official attendants would have to be built in.

Summing up, it should be said that the latest x-ray techniques and research make it easily possible to carry out mass sterilization by means of x-ray; however, it appears to be impossible to take these measures without having those who were to be treated finding out sooner or later that they have been either sterilized or castrated by x-ray."

Brack concluded this letter by asking Himmler what further action could be taken. A subsequent letter was sent to Himmler on June 23, 1942.

Highly esteemed Reichsführer:

Among 10 million European Jews, there are at least two to three million men and women who are in very good condition for performing work. Considering the extraordinary difficulties, which the problem of workers causes us, I suggest we pull out two to three million and keep them alive. However, that is only possible when at the same time they are made sterile.

Approximately a year ago, I reported to you that men especially assigned by me had made the final necessary tests for this purpose. I would like to bring these facts once more back to your memory. Sterilization, as has long been carried out on those afflicted with diseases, is out of the question in this case because it takes too long and is too expensive. Sterilization by means of x-ray, however, is not only relatively inexpensive, but could be carried out on many thousands in the shortest period of time. I also believe that it has become unimportant at this time whether those affected will notice after a few weeks or months that they have been castrated.

In our search for witnesses for the sterilization program described in these letters, we could only come up with two people. Both were boys, sixteen and seventeen years old. One of the two boys was too ill to come to Nuremberg. The other one came. When he came, he was examined by our doctors. I was there during the examination and it was unbelievable. From his waist to just above his knees he was as black as ink, completely burned. He could not stand for more than 15 or 20 minutes. Then he had to sit down. He could only sit down for the same amount of time, 15 or 20 minutes. Then he had to lie down. He could lie down for the same amount of time. Then he had to stand up. That was his routine. He was in excruciating pain. He agreed to testify; however, he said to us he would only testify if his name would not be made public or pictures were taken of him either by still photographers or by television. He was, he explained to us, the sole support of his two little sisters that lived in a town in southern Germany. Well, we told him we could not guarantee it, but we would talk to the judge. We asked for an interview with the judge and we told him what the request was.

The judge listened carefully to their request and said that since they lived in a democracy, he could not ask the newspaper reporters not to report what they heard. "However," said the judge, "I will call them in and tell them the situation and request kindly that they abide by my wishes."

The judge did that and all the correspondents agreed except for one American woman, whose name Fred refused to reveal.

She died long ago. She was a well-known correspondent. She didn't name the person or where he came from, but she wrote an article that a young Jewish boy age 16 appeared as a witness at Nuremberg in the sterilization case. She described him as about 5 feet tall and slender, who came from a small village in southern Germany and who would not give his name, nor did he want to have his picture taken because he was the sole supporter of his two sisters.

I mean, a police report could not have described the man any better than she did. I don't think he [the boy] ever found out what happened. But all the other people in the courtroom, the prosecution team and the other journalists, when we went to the officers' club that evening, avoided her. She became persona non grata among her peers.

The Nazis' reason for medical experiments in general was that it became evident during the war that the Americans had a so-called "wonder drug," namely penicillin. There was no more trench foot or other infectious diseases like during the First World War. The Germans had very little other than sulfa drugs to combat these diseases, so they needed to come up with something like penicillin or something even better. They made numerous experiments, all conducted in a number of different concentration camps, where the people were readily available.

Physicians were there to conduct those experiments, and I want you to understand that some of these physicians were top-notch in their field. Many of them had lectured in the United States. They were not just the average physicians. They were men who had been drafted into the German army, or subsequently into the SS, or were members of the SS to begin with. I'm thinking primarily of others who were the leaders of the SS medical services like Karl Brandt, who later became the personal physician of Hitler; the head of the military medical services and so forth. Others, like Karl

Gebhardt, were very well known for their work with bone diseases and transplantation of bones. Gephardt Rose and Waltheim Sevis both lectured in some of the top universities and medical schools in the United States before the war.

Anyway, they conducted these experiments on inmates who were readily available. One woman was among them, Herta Oberheuser. She too was convicted. Others were good students, like Fritz Fischer, who was a student of Gebhardt, who was an orthopedic man, top in his field, known not only in Germany but also throughout the world. He conducted medical experiments on transplantation of bones. Fischer was his assistant. When he graduated from medical school and was assigned by his professor to work with Gebhardt, he was elated. It would have been just like a medical student who was assigned to work with Cooley or Debakey.

Anyway, he was assigned to him, and after a while he decided that maybe this wasn't right what he was doing. In order to quit his job, he had to apply for a transfer, and the only transfer he could get was to the Russian front. But because he thought the experiments were wrong, he took the transfer, was sent to the Russian front, and lost his arm in combat, which meant that was the end of his career as a surgeon. When we found all the documentation showing that he took part in these experiments, he was indicted, convicted at sentenced to life. The judges took into consideration that he tried to quit and actually did quit,

209

losing his arm as a result. Otherwise he would have gotten the death penalty.

One of the experiments was to cut wounds into people, then insert dirt or glass or anything that would cause an infection, which they would treat with new sulfa drugs. Many of the victims lost their limbs and eventually died because of these experiments.

Other experiments were conducted by Navy personnel, the so-called salt water experiments. They would give people nothing to drink but salt water for longer and longer periods of time. Of course it made them terribly thirsty and many of them also died. Cold water experiments in which men and women were submerged into cold water tanks in increasingly severe conditions until they froze. After they were frozen, they might put men and women together to see if they would revive. I mean they were the most gruesome experiments you can imagine, and they used anybody they could get in the concentration camp — Jews and non-Jews, Gypsies, whoever they could find.

Having had an opportunity to review my numerous interrogations during the trials at Nuremberg, I only know of one case where a criminal admitted that he committed crimes. All others blamed someone else, mostly someone who was no longer alive like Hitler, Göring, Martin Bormann and so on.

I recall one saying, "I did what I did. At the time, I never thought it was wrong. I realize now that it was not only wrong but morally unjust and against my own religious principles. I am willing to take whatever consequences." This individual was Ernst Wilhelm Bohle, who was in charge of all Nazi activities abroad. He held the title of Gauleiter, and had the Germans ever succeeded in coming to America, he would have been in charge of the United States. He was sentenced to a few years in prison.

After Bohle's release, I met with him and his lawyer. He told me that because of what he admitted at the trials he was broke and unable to find a job. He tried to become a salesman for a company. In that capacity, he called one of his former aides, who was by that time the CEO of a major corporation. When he arrived at his fancy offices and asked the CEO's secretary to announce him to his former aide, she came back and told him the CEO, his former aide and friend, would not see traitors. This was the treatment that he received for admitting his errors. Finally, he was selling ladies' underwear and pajamas door to door. He died a few years later. This is just to illustrate what happened to the one guy that I know had told the truth.

Chapter Six

There is a photograph of me at Nuremberg, interrogating Karl Brandt. His attorney and the court reporter were at the table. One guard stood off camera behind me. The interrogation took place at the request of the news media. Brandt, you see, at the end of the Nazi regime, was Hitler's personal physician. The media wanted to know all about Hitler's illnesses.

For me it was a very embarrassing moment. This was the first interrogation of Brandt that I conducted after he had been sentenced to die. The only question I had to ask him was about Hitler's illnesses, all for the gratification of the newspapers and other media of the time. It had nothing to do with the trial.

I asked him, "Since you were so close to Hitler, tell me about his illnesses."

He looked at me and said, "Mr. Rodell, it truly surprises me that you of all people would ask me to do this. All those times while you interrogated me, you repeated over and over the Hippocratic

Oath. Obviously, you're neither a doctor nor a lawyer because if you were you would know that the Hippocratic Oath prevents a physician from discussing the illnesses of his patient. Therefore, there's nothing more I can say to you about this topic."

I just stood there and said, "But your client is dead."

"The Americans never proved that to me," Brandt said.

That was the end of the interrogation; I looked like a fool.

Chapter Seven

Another one of the Nazi leaders who was indicted was Martin Bormann. A Nazi party member since 1925, as I recall, Bormann became very close to Hitler. In fact, he became his closest ally and adviser after Rudolf Hess took off for England. Hess had hoped to negotiate peace with England, but he was arrested there and later brought back to Nuremberg to stand trial with Göring *and the others.*

Bormann, on the other hand, was indicted, tried and sentenced to death in absentia. No one knew where he was; no one could find him.

We obtained some information from the American censorship bureau. They had intercepted a couple of letters. One was from an acquaintance of Bormann, who was in the Merano-Bolzano area in the Dolomite Mountains of northern Italy and claimed to have seen him there. This letter, as I recall, was sent to Munich. The second letter was intercepted coming out of Munich to a person in Sweden, from another acquaintance of Bormann, who claimed to have seen him in that same area up in the mountains. These were the two letters we had, but there were also many rumors linking Bormann to that region. And they made sense. We knew, for instance, that Bormann had a son who was a monk in a monastery in that area.

The third reason we suspected he might be in that region was that he was a known aficionado of Haflinger horses, a special breed from that area. I think he tried to raise them in other parts of Germany but was not successful.

The entire Dolomite region was never occupied by the Allies. As German troops retreated up the Italian boot, they finally surrendered south of Merano-Bolzano. The idea was to surround the mountains and go on with the war. There wasn't a big enough population there to worry about, so no Allied troops had ever gone up. It was left isolated.

When the German SS General Wolff surrendered his troops, he had just received the army payroll. They divided the money for the whole German army in that area among the officers, who then promptly took for the hills.

A different breed of people lived up in these hills. There were no real villages. In one spot you might find a church. Miles away would be a house, miles further away another house. Before World War I, this whole area was part of Austria. The people were German-speaking. They didn't want to speak Italian. They still speak German in that area. They didn't like the Italians very much, and they were very pro-German. So, it was a natural area for these officers to go to hide, not only because they were German, but also because they had a lot of money on them. While touring the area, we came upon a house with a sign in front – Dr.

Somebody. Well, they never had a doctor up there. We found out it was a German army doctor who had decided to hang his shingle out and practice medicine for those people, and they were glad to have him. They never had a doctor before.

The money these German officers carried with them was all in Italian lira, not "occupation money," which made it even easier for them to integrate themselves into the local community without creating a paper trail.

As if this wasn't enough, they had set up a regular courier service, using a sympathetic bus driver, who operated a bus that linked Sweden, Germany and Italy. He carried documents back and forth, getting paid plenty for the service and providing the fugitive German officers with fake Italian identity papers. The people who lived in this region were, after all, Italian citizens whether they liked it or not. So, the region was a perfect hideaway for the Germans.

The people of the Dolomite region were completely self-sufficient. Our guide, Dr. Mobergo, was the head of the Italian resistance for the area. His agents had provided us with the intelligence regarding German activity and the possibility of Bormann's presence. These agents circulated as peddlers, trading items like cloth for food. No money changed hands. Mobergo knew where everybody was up there.

I was assigned by Professor Kempner, who was in charge of the prosecution of different German government ministries at Nuremberg. He knew I spoke both Italian and German and asked me to see what I could find out. "If you find Bormann, see if you can get him to come voluntarily," I remember Kempner saying to me. "If not, arrest him and bring him in."

I contacted Dr. Mobergo, who was anxious to go with me. We had an American jeep with an American driver at our disposal. We drove as far as we could and then we went on foot. It was quite a hike through the mountains to get to the first house.

It is an understatement to say that the people we encountered were not very cooperative. In fact, they were downright hostile, although no one threatened us. You could just see it in their eyes. They wanted nothing to do with our investigation and several doors were slammed in our faces.

Finally, we reached the monastery. It was a place right out of the Middle Ages surrounded by a moss-covered wall. We knew Bormann's son was a monk inside these walls. We hoped to be invited in, but we never were. The first monk came out and I asked to see the abbot, who was the monastery's superior cleric. He came out after a short while, and I asked if I could speak to Martin Bormann's son. He simply shook his head and said no, I could not.

I told him that we had information suggesting that Bormann, himself, was in the area. The abbot shrugged and said he didn't know. Taking note that this so-called holy man seemed disinterested in cooperating with us, I took a different approach.

I said, "What would you do if Hitler or Himmler came to your monastery seeking sanctuary?"

He said, "Let me tell you, my job is to give a home to the homeless and food to the hungry."

"So, if Hitler came up, what would you do?"

"I give a home to the homeless, and food to the hungry, that's all I can tell you." With that, he slammed the door in my face, and I had no choice but to leave.

Finally, Dr. Mobergo and I found ourselves on top of a

217

small hill not far from the monastery. "It's obvious we're not getting anywhere," Mobergo said. "I say we leave. But first I want you to wait for me here while I go run a quick errand."

I couldn't imagine what sort of errand Dr. Mobergo needed to run in a place where we were obviously not welcome. But I agreed to wait and made myself comfortable. He was gone nearly two hours. I was sitting there staring in the direction he had gone, hoping to see him appear along the trail, when suddenly I heard a couple of shots fired from a pistol. A short time later Mobergo appeared.

"What happened?" I asked him. "I heard some shots."

Mobergo shrugged. "Don't worry," he said rather casually. "It's just one less Nazi in this world."

I could not persuade him to elaborate.

I returned to Nuremberg empty handed. Over the years that followed there were numerous rumors about Bormann, some saying he was indeed in the Dolomite region, others suggesting that he had died with Hitler in Berlin. The truth may never be known.

Bormann was, however, tried in absentia. The attorney assigned to defend him was Dr. Friedrich Bergold, an old friend of my family, who I had known all my life. His father had been a close friend of my father. Neither Dr. Bergold, nor his father, nor any of the members of their family were ever Nazis. Bergold served in the German army and, upon his return to Nuremberg after the war, attempted to revive his law practice. It was nearly impossible for him to get work, until he was assigned to defend Bormann. Although he found the job distasteful, he was lucky in that there was no one to actually defend – his client was not around.

After the trial, I met with him many times. He told me he

needed more work and wondered if I knew of any not-so-bad Nazis who needed a defender. I wasn't able to help him. Years later, I learned that after the trials Dr. Bergold was able to go back to work and became a very successful lawyer.

Not too long ago, I heard that Dr. Bergold had passed away in Nuremberg. He was more or less my same age.

Chapter Eight

I want to come to something else. I haven't said much about General Donovan, who during WWI acquired the nickname of Wild Bill. He was the recipient of the most medals awarded to any U.S. soldier during World Wars I and II. Among the many medals he received was the Congressional Medal of Honor.

In civilian life, he was a well-known and highly respected lawyer, the head of a major law firm that had offices in New York, Washington, Chicago, London and Paris. In 1932 he was a Republican and unsuccessfully ran for governor of New York. Prior to WWII, he went on a number of fact-finding missions for President Roosevelt throughout the world. Roosevelt called him in one of his speeches my "eyes and ears in the world," in spite of the fact that he was a Republican and Roosevelt was a Democrat. They went to college together, knew each other well and had respect for each other.

Donovan was without a doubt not only the most respected officer among of the members of O.S.S., but he was truly beloved by everyone that knew him. The way he treated us, the way he ran the organization... it was just unbelievable.

I recently tracked down a photograph of my wife Sheryl, Donovan and me when he came to Houston at the invitation of the Junior Chamber of Commerce. In the early 1950s living in Houston and having been in business in Houston, I was a member and belonged to one of the international committees. Each year we arranged an annual meeting. One day a friend of mine, Art Riklin, who was chairman of the committee, came to my office and said: "During the war, you were in the service." Yes.

"You served in the O.S.S." Yes.

"Do you know a fellow by the name of General Donavan?" Yes, why?

"Because he was invited by some of the big shots from the Chamber, the Mayor's office and religious leaders to come speak, but none of them have received a reply. Can you write to him and see if he can come or if we have to find someone else?"

I said I'd be glad to do it, but if you want me to I'd call him. He said, "Do you know him that well?"

I said, well, yes, but I think he knows me a lot better than I know him.

I picked up the phone and called his office at Number Two Wall Street. The young lady who answered was named Rose, and I knew her well. She recognized me. I said I'd like to speak to the general if he was there. She said, just a moment, then suddenly, he came on the phone and said, "Fred, what the hell are you doing in Texas?" I said, well, I live down here now, I'm married and I'm in business.

The general congratulated me and then said, "So what can I do for you?"

"Well, I have a gentleman with me from the City of Houston Junior Chamber of Commerce, and he tells me that they invited you to be the keynote speaker at their annual meeting, and they haven't received a response. They want to know whether you're coming or not."

The general remembered having seen something and admitted that he hadn't answered yet. But he said, "You can tell them for me, that if I can spend some time with my boy Fred, and meet his wife, I'll be there. Accept the invitation for me; tell them I'll be contacting you with my arrival information."

"I'll be happy to meet you at the airport," I said. "And I'll be at your service from the time you get here until you leave Houston. I'm really looking forward to seeing you again, sir."

"I'm looking forward to seeing you too, Fred," he said. "Goodbye, son."

"Goodbye, sir."

And that was the end of the conversation.

Shortly thereafter, I got a message from him telling me what flight he was on. My wife Sheryl and I went to the airport, where we met him. It was quite a reunion for me since I hadn't seen him in a number of years. We took him to his hotel, the Warwick, and went out to dinner that night in the restaurant downstairs. The next day was the dinner, at River Oaks Country Club in Houston. We picked him up and accompanied him to the annual meeting. I was amazed at how much he really knew about me, as he kept telling my wife things that I had long forgotten. Some of the very things I've told you and you've written down, General Donovan remembered about me from my years with the OSS. And I was just

222

one of the many thousands of members. I always had the highest regard for the General. He was one of the most admirable men that I ever knew.

As we drove to the airport to bid goodbye to him, he said to my wife, "Mrs. Rodell, I asked Fred to send me a copy of his current resumé, and he said yes, but I have the feeling he has no intention of doing so. I wish you would see to it that he does. Will you do that for me?"

I said, "General, I have no qualms about sending you my resume. You know all about me anyway. I just want to make sure that it doesn't get any kind of preferred status in any future wars."

He said, "Son, let me tell you something," and he put his hand on my shoulder. "If there is another war, and God knows I'm an old man now, they may call me and you and others like us to serve. I just want to have your information handy so I can gather my team together again."

Naturally, I agreed to send it. And that unfortunately was the last time I saw General Donavan.

He had just returned from having been Ambassador to Thailand. He died at Walter Reed Hospital in Washington on February 8, 1959. It was rather sad because he was in an advanced state of Alzheimer's disease. One time they found him wandering the streets of Washington in his pajamas. His memory was gone.

He was a kind man who seldom got angry. I don't know of anyone who ever saw him in a rage. I don't think he ever spoke a foul word to anyone. He always had a smile on his face. I'll never forget his sparkling grey eyes.

The general is buried in Arlington National Cemetery.

Postscript

International Military Tribunal at Nuremberg

Beginning in the winter of 1942, the governments of the Allied powers announced their determination to punish Nazi war criminals.

On Dec. 17, 1942, leaders of the U.S., Great Britain and the Soviet Union issued the first joint declaration officially noting the mass murder of European Jewry and resolving to prosecute those responsible for violence against civilian populations. Though some political leaders advocated summary executions instead of trials, eventually the Allies decided to hold an International Military Tribunal.

The trials of leading German officials before the International Military Tribunal (IMT) formally opened in Nuremberg, Germany, on Nov. 20, 1945, only six and a half months after Germany surrendered. Each of the four Allied nations supplied a judge and a prosecution team. A team of translators provided simultaneous translations of all proceedings in four languages: English, French, German, and Russian.

Twenty-four defendants were selected to represent a cross-section of Nazi diplomatic, economic, political and military leadership. Adolf Hitler, Heinrich Himmler and Joseph Goebbels never stood trial, having committed suicide before the end of the war, so only 21 defendants appeared in court.

The IMT indicted the defendants on charges of crimes against peace, war crimes and crimes against humanity. The IMT defined crimes against humanity as "murder, extermination, enslavement, deportation...or persecutions on political, racial, or religious grounds." A fourth charge of conspiracy was added both to cover crimes committed under domestic Nazi law before the start of World War II and so that subsequent tribunals would have jurisdiction to prosecute any individual belonging to a proven criminal organization. The defendants were entitled to a legal counsel of their choosing.

American chief prosecutor Robert Jackson decided to argue his case primarily on the basis of mounds of documents written by the Nazis themselves rather than eyewitness testimony, so that the trial could not be accused of relying on biased or tainted testimony. Testimony presented at Nuremberg revealed much of what is known about the Holocaust.

The judges delivered their verdict on October 1, 1946. Twelve defendants were sentenced to death, among them Joachim von Ribbentrop, Hans Frank, Alfred Rosenberg and Julius Streicher. They were hanged, cremated in Dachau, and their ashes dropped in the Isar River. Hermann Goering escaped the hangman's noose by committing suicide the night before. The IMT sentenced three defendants to life imprisonment and four to prison terms ranging from 10 to 20 years. It acquitted three of the defendants.

The IMT trial at Nuremberg was just one of the earliest and most famous of several subsequent war crimes trials. The overwhelming majority of post-1945 war crimes trials involved lower-level officials and officers.

Other war criminals were tried by the courts of those countries where they had committed their crimes. In 1947, a court in Poland sentenced Auschwitz camp commandant Rudolf Hoess to death. In the courts of West Germany, many former Nazis did not receive severe sentences, with the claim of following orders from superiors often ruled a mitigating circumstance. A number of Nazi criminals therefore returned to normal lives in German society, especially in the business world.

The efforts of Nazi hunters (such as Simon Wiesenthal and Beate Klarsfeld) led to the capture, extradition, and trial of a number of Nazis who had escaped from Germany after the war. Many war criminals, however, were never brought to trial or punished.

(Source: U.S. Holocaust Museum)

William J. "Wild Bill" Donovan with Sheryl Rodell and Fred Rodell in Houston, 1950

Fred Rodell (right) interrogates Dr. Karl Brandt, Hitler's personal physician (second from left).

Dr. Karl Brandt on trial at Nuremberg, 1947

Fred Rodell researching Nuremberg records and photos, 1995

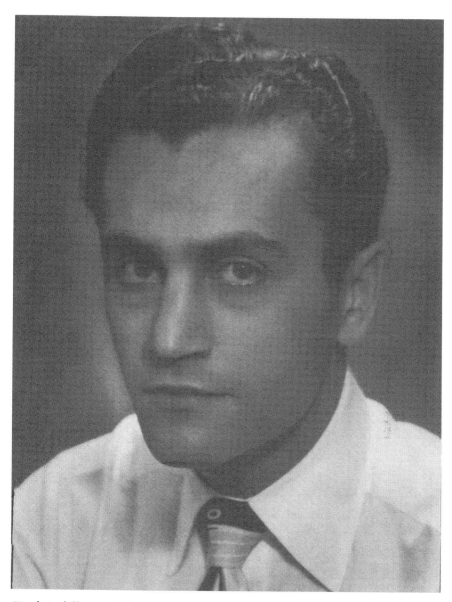

Fred Rodell in 1946

Acknowledgements

This book would not have been possible without the support, guidance and assistance of many people. First and foremost, I thank my beautiful wife Ellen for always being there for me and making sure I had what I needed to keep plugging away at a work that, in the end, took more than 20 years to complete. Ellen and I paid several visits to Fred and Sheryl at their home in Lakeway, Texas, and we saw Fred together for the last time when we attended his July 4, 2000 birthday party in Austin.

My brothers John and Michael both served as proofreaders and editors of early manuscripts and definitely left their mark on the finished product. John passed a copy of the manuscript to his colleague at Gateway College in Connecticut – Professor Emeritus Russell Gaudio – who provided many notes on the text, editing suggestions and encouraging comments.

My colleague Jan Hester had an enormous impact on the book as an exceptional editor and the driving force behind both the *Timeline of Holocaust and World War II* and all of the historical notes throughout the book.

Andre Edwin, my longtime friend and a talented writer, read and provided his thoughts on at least two early versions of the manuscript. I'm looking forward to doing the same for Andre when he is ready to let me read his third book already in progress.

And finally I thank my three daughters, Carmen, Ashley and Isabella and my new baby granddaughter Aria for being my inspiration to keep writing.

64427222R00133

Made in the USA
Middletown, DE
13 February 2018